THE Christmas Cook

A MERRY CHRISTMAS

Also by William Woys Weaver

A Quaker Woman's Cookbook
Sauerkraut Yankees
Thirty-five Receipts
America Eats

THE Christmas Cook

Three Centuries of American Yuletide Sweets

WILLIAM WOYS WEAVER

PHOTOGRAPHY BY JERRY ORABONA

HarperPerennial
A Division of HarperCollins*Publishers*

FRONTISPIECE: Packages wrapped with sealing wax and colored
string, a gingerbread elephant, and Peanut Taffy (PAGE 207) re-
create details from a Christmas Eve a century ago.

THE CHRISTMAS COOK. Copyright © 1990 by William Woys Weaver. All rights reserved. Printed
in Hong Kong by South China Printing Company. No part of this book may be used or reproduced
in any manner whatsoever without written permission except in the case of brief quotations
embodied in critical articles and reviews. For information address HarperCollins Publishers,
10 East 53rd Street, New York, NY 10022.

First HarperPerennial Edition

DESIGNED BY JOEL AVIROM

Library of Congress Cataloging-in-Publication Data

Weaver, William Woys, 1947–
The Christmas cook: three centuries of American Yuletide sweets/William Woys Weaver.
p. cm.
Includes bibliographical references.
ISBN 0-06-055212-3
ISBN 0-06-096552-5 (pbk.)
1. Christmas cookery. 2. Desserts. 3. Confectionery. 4. Cookery, American. I. Title.
TX739.2.C45W4 1990 89-49170
641.5′68—dc20

90 91 92 93 94 10 9 8 7 6 5 4 3 2 1

90 91 92 93 94 10 9 8 7 6 5 4 3 2 1 (pbk.)

For Gertrud and Heinz Benker,
a nod across the Atlantic, in
remembrance of the magic at
Schloss Buchenau

Contents

Traditional Recipes

Tested for the Modern Kitchen

Traditional Recipes Tested for the Modern Kitchen

Acknowledgments

Books are the product of many busy hands, so it is only proper that I begin by acknowledging the corporate hands of the many institutions that allowed me to cite or reproduce material in their collections. In particular, I would like to mention the Art Institute of Chicago; the Chester County Historical Society, West Chester, Pennsylvania; the Deutsches Brodmuseum in Ulm, Germany; Doe Run Valley Books of Chadds Ford, Pennsylvania; the Henry Francis DuPont Winterthur Museum, Winterthur, Delaware; the Kulturgeschichtliches Museum Osnabrück, Osnabrück, Germany; the Library Company of Philadelphia; the Library of Congress; the Philadelphia Museum of Art; the University of South Carolina Press; the Van Pelt Library of the University of Pennsylvania; the Wyck Association of Philadelphia; and the York Castle Museum, York, England.

Among the private individuals who assisted me, I would like to single out writer Gertrud Benker and her husband Heinz, a well-known Munich composer. Gertrud was gracious enough to take time off from her own book writing and offer me tireless help in locating material, in permitting me to invade her library, in putting me up as a house guest, in baking me countless apple strudels conjured from the apple tree in her yard, and in carting me about the Bavarian countryside to visit craftspersons and significant culinary sites, not the least being Schloss Buchenau, the home of the late food writer Erna Horn, where Heinz improvised an extraordinary polonaise on an equally extraordinary Bösendorfer. As for Heinz, we share the same birthday and a mutual love for Bacchus.

Likewise, I want to thank another fellow tippler, Rudolf Garo of Zürich. Friend and folklorist-turned-banker, Rudi was particularly generous with his time and hospitality in showing me the food scene in his country —the land of my own ancestral roots.

I must also mention Hans Staib of Ulm, Germany, who not only permitted me to tour his bakery but also made for me several springerle cookies from rare molds in his famous collection, among them the 1642 Nativity scene on page 125.

Charles Regennas of Lititz, Pennsylvania, did the same with the clear toys shown in this book. Each candy was made by hand from nineteenth-century molds in his outstanding collection. Charles may be the last of the small "family" confectioners; his candy shop on Lemon Street in Lititz is a mecca not just for children in the neighborhood but also for lovers of old-time Christmas from all over the country.

I also want to mention David Houston, the able pastry chef at Ridgewell's in King of Prussia, Pennsylvania, who good-naturedly accepted my last-minute pleas and did his best to assemble the Twelfth Night Cake on page 4 and style it as I directed after an 1850s woodcut.

Then there is my friend James Gergat of Maple on the Hill Antiques in Avondale, Pennsylvania, who lent me innumerable objects for the photography. So too did Susan Lucas—literally several cartons of family heirlooms. But Susan also came by daily during the photography sessions to help me prepare food, run errands, and to clean up the devastation in my kitchen. I could not have survived it without her.

This brings me to the photography itself, a happy marriage of temperaments and art brought about by Barbara Gold, the heroine of a circuitous story that began with a postcard view of decaying pears. Never mind the pears or the Rembrandt shadows, she found Jerry Orabona for me and he did wonders with my food. His camera, or should I say the Orabona Eye, saw a world of light and shadow that came very close to me in spirit. For that I shall remain eternally amazed.

I also want to thank Patrick F. Raccioppi of Tappan, New York, an able photographer in his own right, who assisted Jerry so patiently and so expertly on site and in the studio.

Finally, I want to extend my heartiest thanks to Joel Avirom for giving my book an elegant design that captures the magic of Christmas.

—*William Woys Weaver*

Acknowledgments

THE Christmas Cook

Introduction

"Christmas is coming, and the holidays are coming, and all the children are coming, and all the grand-children are coming, and all their country cousins are coming, and all their uncles and aunts are coming, and every one of these wants their share of Christmas goodies, the Christmas eating and Christmas drinking, the Christmas pies, cakes, puddings and Christmas confections; its bon-bons, nicknacks, and its forty thousand sweet things."

—JAMES W. PARKINSON
"Christmas Good Cheer," *The Confectioners' Journal*, December 1877.

Regardless of where Americans may be in the world, on December 25 we eat. Behind this habit of holiday indulgence stretches a long and convoluted history, half myth, half fact, that has shaped our inner picture of this feast. From an intellectual standpoint, especially from the standpoint of a writer like me, who grew up in a religious tradition that historically rejected it, Christmas is utterly unassailable, enveloped in a protective shell of goodwill all of its own making. Why? Because Christmas is an emotion that exists beyond the purely rational; it is a sense of well-being and goodness that illuminates a light within us.

Thus, the best way for me to characterize *The Christmas Cook* is to describe it as a holiday lantern that shines into the shady recesses of history, casting long shadows perhaps, but also dropping patches of light on the old and noble art of sharing at table. In my role as Professor Christmas, I have tried to sort out the distinct historical phases that our Christmas has passed through, the various changes in its character, and the foods that made it so. In addition, I have gathered together the best or the most representative recipes, and after five years of testing and tasting, I have translated them into modern equivalents as true to the originals as possible. I think the selection is so complete that you may consider this nearly as good as anything Mother Christmas will tell you herself. And even if you are the sort who never goes near the stove, at least you may consider this your candy-store guide to rare views and old utensils that are every bit as fascinating as the food. In my work as a food historian and consultant I am bombarded daily with inquiries from housewives, professional cooks, other writers, the news media, and the food industry. To a large extent, I have answered many of the questions most often asked about Christmas cookery in the pages of this book. Thus, there is something in it for everyone, something for the professional chef as well as the inexperienced cook.

On the other hand, I have not attempted to make this a total guide to holiday dining, even though I have made some effort to discuss Christmas menus, that is, meals as a whole. This is a book about dessert cookery, particularly the traditional fare. In colonial America, much attention was lavished on the dessert course. We have always placed great emphasis on this part of our meals, and this is perhaps where we shine most in home cookery. The dessert course became the natural frame for *The Christmas Cook*.

Perhaps there is a companion volume waiting to be written on the meat and vegetable dishes served at Christmas, but it will never be quite as thick as this one. The reason is simple: Americans developed a somewhat standardized roast goose or roast turkey dinner in the eighteenth century and have stuck to that formula more or less ever since. It is in our Christmas desserts and in our decorative foods that we have shown greatest ingenuity and variety.

Even though we are a nation with a penchant for desserts, we also have become increasingly conscious about nutrition. Well, we give it plenty of lip service. And as far as diets are concerned, we are cagier than the CIA in our undercover cheating. Let's be frank. If you exercise regularly and maintain a reasonable diet during the rest of the year, no harm will come to you from eating a few Christmas cookies or even a guiltless slice of plum pudding, suet and all.

Keep in mind that early Americans ate rather spartan meals most of the time, consumed lots of whole grains, worked hard, and reserved the rich foods for only a handful of special occasions. We tend to think of the ostentatious meals of bloated nineteenth-century robber barons when we think of Christmas past—an image promoted by Hollywood—but in truth, things were generally much simpler and far less deadly. You may be surprised to learn that some of my oldest and tastiest recipes can pass as vegetarian— Methodist Mincemeat and Cranberry Flummery among them. Others are low in fat or low in sugar, and a great many are completely salt free.

Lastly, this is a book with a mission. Through my narratives and my recipes, I want to share with you the great riches of our American heritage; I have always felt that when we understand a thing better, we enjoy it twice as much. I also want to give you the tools and the insight to go further than this book, to transform what you have read here into a living tradition in your own home.

In short, I have tried to give you a cupboard of ideas brimming over with pies and cakes, puddings and confections, bonbons and Nic-Nacs, and well nigh forty thousand sweet things. The images are endless: the marzipan figures, the tree sparkling with barley sugar, the drifts of cookies tumbling like small avalanches into the mouths of merry little faces, the dining room transformed into a candycane landscape, where even the clumsiest gingerbread creatures can dance and sing. Why do we love this? Because it makes us happy.

PAGE xvi:

An angel made with the Yule Dollie recipe (PAGE 127) accents an arrangement of eighteenth- and nineteenth-century cookies: Chocolate Apeas, Almond Macaroons, Gingerbread (with the basket design), Honey Cake with snowflake icing, and a border of Marmalade of Quinces in the shape of rings.

Introduction

Bringing in Christmas

For many religious denominations, Christmas Day was set aside for sermonizing and prayer, and little else. Much to the irritation of this quiet faction, *other* Christians chose to make noise. Mary Boardman Crowninshield, proper New Englander and wife of the secretary of the navy, noted in her diary for Christmas 1815: "Christmas morn. It seems more like our Independence—guns firing all night."[1] New Englander that she was, she chose to go to Catholic church in Washington, D.C.—where she lived—because "it is their great day." In any case, Christmas revelry, or "making the night hideous" to those who did not approve, was an integral part of the American celebration of the holiday.[2] And with it came a vast array of foods whose origins stretched back into the early Middle Ages, in some cases into the pre-Christian era.

Christmas mumming preserved many of these food customs—such as the serving of boar's head and the drinking of wassail—and gave names to a number of Christmas dishes. Mumming was essentially a reenactment of popular stories or folk tales based on Christmas themes in which the participants dressed in fantastic or comic costumes. Masking was essential because the participants were expected to assume a new identity, or at least for the moment to free

Twelfth Night Cake decorated with fondant roses (see the Potato Fondant recipe on PAGE 197) and a paste sugar cherub replicates a cake from an 1850s cookbook. Near the rose champagne, a dish of New Years Crackers and Nic-Nacs invite the party revelers.

"Bringing in Christmas" from an 1864 wood engraving. (Roughwood Collection)

haps also a touch of well-earned gluttony. Individuals joined the merrymaking, not as part of a family unit but along broader lines of gender, age group, and marital status. These divisions were evident in the choice of costumes and in seating arrangements at the common table.

In some sections of America where the Church of England was strong, as for example in Virginia, Christmas revelry on the plantations often took the form of mumming, after the fashion of Old England. This mumming sometimes followed the loose format of a children's play based on the folk *Play of St. George*.[3] The list of characters was as long as the ingenuity of the mummers, but inevitably the play featured a representation of Father Christmas. His counterpart was Old Bett or Betty, the vernacular name for Mother Christmas, a role often assumed by one of the black boys in the house. From this comes *Brown Betty,* a comic children's term for the apple pudding presented as a symbolic gift to the mummers from the *old lady.* There is a recipe for Brown Betty at the end of this chapter.

Another figure from this medieval theme was Jack, a personality generally portrayed as a humpback, an idiot, or a cripple, but who was nevertheless the real court jester of the group. Dandy Jack was his variation, a clown who was ladylike. During the nineteenth century, his name was extended in the South to include blackface as well as black comics, with the connotation of being

themselves of their own. In England, this type of feasting was communal in that the entire village or town participated. The whole community moved into the local castle or manor house and transformed the great hall into a scene of mirth, revelry, and per-

overly grand, overly mannered, and overly effeminate. He survives in the name of a Christmas poverty dish of the South called Dandy Jack Pudding. Jack Pudding, incidentally, was another old English name for a mummer, just as *Hanswurst* was the same type of clown in Germany.[4]

I should also add here that the use of blackface by the mummers was not originally a parody of blacks. Persons who could not procure mumming masks rubbed their faces with soot, a variant form of masking that traces its roots deep into the Middle Ages. It also appears among the Pennsylvania Germans, who mummed, or in their terms *belschnickeled,* on Second Christmas, the general market day observed on December 26.[5]

Both the blackface and the elaborate masked costumes appear in the New Years Day mumming that takes place in Philadel-

The Cuckold, or "Unable" Husband, a comic figure in
Christmas mumming. Speculatius mold, nineteenth century.

phia each year—one of the few places in the country where this tradition has been carried down to the present. The true definition of mumming on the Calends of January, as practiced by the Romans to celebrate the end of their ten-month year, was a reversal of roles—men dressing as women, slaves portrayed as masters, old men acting as babies, children passing for adults. The Christian church was never comfortable with this form of merrymaking because it often went beyond mere masking and encouraged lewd behavior that the church expressly forbid.

Since blackface was an acceptable form of masking, mumming in America did not always imply a costume or even a fanciful mask. In fact, there could be no outward form of costume. As in the case of the drawing of Christmas mumming on the Kansas frontier in 1857 illustrated on the opposite page, the children (of both races) have assumed the roles of imaginary musicians, which they are acting out with great vigor on old pots and pans. This particular game or skit was known as "Marching in Christmas," and it continued as a folk custom well into the end of the nineteenth century.

Impersonations also took other forms, as for example in the shapes of foods exchanged during the season. One of the most ancient of these was the *yule dow* or *yule dough,* a pastry image given out by bakers at Christmas.[6] This custom survived in America in several forms: in stamped pictorial New Years cookies; in shaped, decorated gingerbread cookies; in crullers cut into figures; and in such image cookies as the Yule Dollies discussed in chapter 5.

Medieval yule *dows* generally depicted animals or human figures, especially the Baby Jesus. In the nineteenth century, with the renewal of interest in medieval Christmas customs, *dows* were revived as doll cookies, hence Yule Dollies. Yule Dollies often depicted romantic Victorian historical themes.

Pulcinella or Punch, depicted here as a hand puppet. Tin cookie cutter, nineteenth century. (Philadelphia Museum of Art)

The Christmas Cook

Christmas mumming in Kansas, 1857. (Roughwood Collection)

In this country, commercial Yule Dollies were commonly sold in the shape of girls in tall hats and long dresses reminiscent of the picturesque "folk" costume of Wales developed during the 1800s to spur Welsh tourism.[7] In short, one anachronism imitated the other.

Dow-knots were yet another variant of *yule dough,* being bows, wreaths, and other intricate shapes fried in deep fat. The most common shape in home cookery, however, was a simple ring, hence the vernacular name *fried jumble.* Jumbles are an extremely ancient shape in pastry; the name implies a ring shape only, not a specific recipe. Since the word is a corruption of Latin *gemel,* meaning twin, the original form may have resembled two ropes of dough twisted into a ring.

Doughnuts, the most common American name for the fried rings, are still a popular festive food in parts of New England and elsewhere. Commercialization has now made doughnuts available year round and de-

Cookie cutter depicting a Welsh folk costume, circa 1899, and Yule Dollie ornamented with icing, feather, and scrap picture face.

prived them of their original holiday context. Yule doughs, like doughnuts, were also sometimes referred to as *Baby Cakes,* just as in German similar gift foods were called *Christkindeln. Baby Cake* was a designation for any cakes or cookies that served as gift foods at Christmas, the implication being that they were special gifts of the Christ Child. In Anglo-American folk culture, Baby Cake was also one of the characters in Christmas and Twelfth Night mummings.

TWELFTH NIGHT AND ITS RELATED CUSTOMS

One of the primary activities of the Romans and Greeks on January 1 was to exchange gifts in order to renew old friendships. The *xenia,* as this exchange was called, was a means of recementing political relationships, reaffirming family connections, remembering lovers, and reoiling the bonds of financial arrangements. In colonial America, the New Years gift for a long time received far more emphasis than the distribution of gifts at Christmas.

Christmas gifts were generally small and symbolic, a sprig of gilded rosemary or a gilded nutmeg, an apple stuck with a sprig of fresh rosemary, an orange or lemon stuck with cloves, a marzipan figure or perhaps a Baby Cake. At New Years, however, moralizing books for children, a purse, a trinket box, or some other object of continued usefulness might be given out during open house as a reminder that New Years was a clean slate for self-improvement. We should not forget that this exchange was accompanied by plenty of ale, hard cider, wine, punch,

The Christmas Cook

hypocras, and especially at New Years, a *slabby* (thick) drink variously called *Lamb's Tongue* or *Lamb's Wool*.[8] *Lamb's Wool* is a corruption of *lammas-owel,* originally a pre-Christian drink served at the Festival of Lughnasa on August 1—the ceremonial beginning of the Celtic harvest. In England, this beverage is now more generally known by its Anglo-Saxon name: wassail. Traditionally, wassail was served in a wooden bowl.

An old New Years song from Gloucestershire mentioned a wassail bowl made of maple.[9] One wonders how many of the old burly maple bowls that turn up on the antiques market in this country may have served this happy function. We do know from a Philadelphia newspaper advertisement in the 1730s that wooden punch bowls were in large demand for the country trade.[10] And no wonder. Due to the rounds of hospitality between Christmas and New Years, the exchange of courtesy gifts and merry drinking continued intermittently from December 25 until Twelfth Night Eve.

Yule Dows stuck with sprigs of fresh and gilded rosemary.

Twelfth Night was most faithfully observed in Virginia, Maryland, Delaware, and Pennsylvania among the Church of England people and by wealthy families in general who often used it as a pretext for holding a ball. A Twelfth Night ball raised expectations that there would be a Twelfth Night Cake and an extraordinary array of foods to eat, and that there probably would be some form of mumming or masking in addition to dancing. Many American Twelfth Night balls were restricted to the young and the unmarried; this was their annual opportunity to mingle freely and if cupid would have it, to make their move.

Bridget Ann Henisch has written a full and well-illustrated history of Twelfth Night feasting that now supercedes previous research, except for the American side of the story, for which material is admittedly scant.[11] I have tried to sketch in a little more on our custom because much of it centers on foods for which I have discovered many early recipes.

William Byrd, a Virginian, celebrated Twelfth Night after dinner in 1740 in a manner typical for rural families in the South: "I talked to my people, drew twelfth cake, gave the people cake and cider, and prayed."[12] His "people" in this case were his house servants. One gathers from first impression that this was a rather low-key affair for Byrd, but doubtless for his slaves, a slice of rich fruit cake and a nip of hard cider (all cider was drunk hard in this period) was indeed a rare

way to cap an evening. On the other hand, Byrd's prayerful finish to Twelfth Night was hardly typical. We know from other parts of his diary that he often fell into such fits of prayer after he had committed some amorous transgression—a commentary perhaps about the way in which he himself had passed the day. His guilt, incidentally, rarely lasted much longer than an evening.

Twelfth Night Cake, Christmas Cake, Great Cake, Plum Cake—these were all synonyms for the large fruitcake that Byrd served at his little gathering. An unusual recipe by the name of Twelfth Cake is preserved in the *American Family Cook Book* of 1858, in which sawdust is scattered in the pan under the cake "to prevent the bottom from coloring too much" during its four-hour baking.[13] The result is a huge cake twelve to fourteen inches high. There was evidently considerable status attached to the size of one's Twelfth Night Cake, never mind the difficulties in baking it. The recipe I have included in this chapter is a bit more manageable and one that is so popular with my friends I was once asked to bake four for a wedding! My secret comes from Frederic Nutt's *Complete Confectioner* published at New York in 1807, a book widely used at the time by bakeshops in this country.

Regarding Twelfth Night Cake, there is an important point of procedure that must not be overlooked because it is the one feature that differentiates this cake from your general run of fruitcake: a bean and a pea should be mixed into the batter before the cake is baked, and they should be large enough that they do not disappear into the other ingredients during baking. This feature is important not only because it ostensibly brings luck to those who find the bean and pea, it is also the mechanism by which the party is carried forward to its next level of merriment: choosing a king and queen.

The king and queen were determined by either finding the bean or pea in the cake—for king and queen respectively, by drawing slips of paper with names written on them, or by drawing picture cards depicting Twelfth Night characters, which one then assumed in the form of mumming or a masquerade. It was a parlor game of sorts designed to get everyone involved and matched off for the dancing, lest shy ones hang back along the edges of the party.

The Twelfth Night Cake made a great appearance on the table and was doubtless one of the most festive objects in the room because it was heavily iced and ornamented with elaborate sugarwork figures. The only region of the country where this custom still survives is Louisiana, where the cake is known popularly as *gâteau du roi*. It is served from Twelfth Night to Mardi Gras.[14] However, references do turn up in other places.

In the correspondence of Sarah Bethel Kuhn of Lancaster, Pennsylvania, there is a series of letters in 1785 describing a famous Twelfth Night ball at Miss Hoofnagle's in the Borough, for which most of the ladies made new gowns. On page 14 I have reproduced three Twelfth Night ball invitations from the 1790s similar to those sent out in 1785. They were printed on playing cards, which was the fashion in this period. Dicing and card games of course were part of normal Twelfth Night festivities.

Sarah Kuhn described the ball to her mother a few days later: "We had a very grand 'Twelfth' indeed, too great a profusion of victuals was the only fault. The Doctor [Kuhn's husband] had the honor, as they call it, to draw 'King' tho it was what we had no ambition for. Mrs. Moore was Queen."[15]

As for the victuals, one can imagine the tables set up as *ambigues,* or in modern terms, set up buffet-style in the round, as described in greater detail on pages 215–216. Everything was laid out in geometric order so that all the fine china platters, the glass stands, and the silver serving dishes balanced out among the pyramids of glacé fruits and pastry work cornucopias, the greenery, and the gleaming candles.

This type of menu was taken to task by many Protestant reformers in the early nineteenth century. Mordecai Noah's sputtering indignation is typical:

What a sum to be destroyed in one short hour! The *substantials* on this table, consisting of a few turkeys, tongues, hams, fowls, rounds of beef and game, all cold, could have been purchased for *fifty dollars;* the

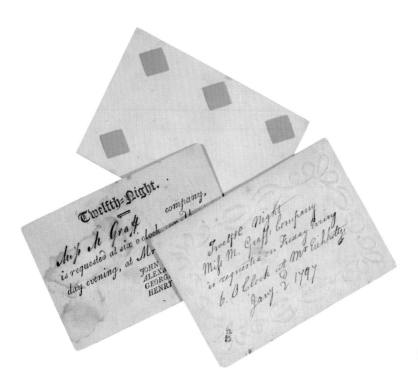

Invitations to Twelfth Night parties held at Lancaster, Pennsylvania, in 1796 and 1797. After the fashion of the period, these invitations were printed on blank playing cards. (Roughwood Collection)

residue of this immense sum was expended for whips, creams, floating islands, pyramids of kisses, temples of sugarplumbs, ices, *blanc manges,* macaroons and plumb cake; and ladies of delicacy, of refined habits, of soft and amiable manners, were, *at midnight,* cloying their stomachs, after excessive exercise in dancing, with this trash.[16]

Alas, our trash piles up quickly because there are a good many more delectables that Mr. Noah overlooked: Wafers and Jelly, a sideboard setpiece; Orange Fritters with port wine sauce, a true luxury in the days when oranges were both scarce and expen-sive, even in port towns; and from western Virginia and Tennessee, Twelfth Night Wafers, a rich sugar cookie similar to a sand tart that certainly would have given the man apoplexy considering the number of eggs required to make one batch. Then there is New Years Pie, in which a beef tongue is stuffed into a boned chicken, and the boned chicken stuffed into a boned duck, and the duck stuffed into a boned turkey, and the turkey stuffed into a boned goose, which is then seasoned and baked and, when cold, encased in a molded aspic.[17] At a cost that would otherwise feed a family of six for a month, I doubt you are likely to make it.

DANDY JACK PUDDING

1874

YIELD: 6 SERVINGS.

4 eggs, separated
1 quart milk
1 cup plus 3 tablespoons superfine sugar

3 tablespoons all-purpose flour
1½ tablespoons vanilla extract or 1¼ teaspoon lemon extract

*P*reheat the oven to 350°F.

Beat the egg yolks with 1 cup of milk, then sift in 1 cup of the sugar. Beat until the sugar is dissolved. Add the flour and beat until all lumps are gone. Scald the remaining 3 cups of milk and add it to the mixture. Pour this into a heavy saucepan and bring it to a gentle boil. Whisk vigorously until thick, then add the extract. Pour into a two-quart custard or soufflé dish. Beat the egg whites until stiff, sweeten with the remaining sugar, and spread over the pudding. Set in the preheated oven for 10 minutes, or until the meringue turns golden. Cool at room temperature, then refrigerate. Serve when cold.

NOTE: This can also be prepared in 2 prebaked 9-inch pie shells.

SOURCE: *Hoofland's Almanac and Family Receipt Book for Everybody's Use* (Philadelphia: Johnston, Holloway & Co., 1874), unpaginated.

Dandy Jack as Santa Claus. The bicycle wheel is intended to create the illusion of a halo. Chromolithograph by Louis Prang & Co., Boston, Christmas 1881. (Courtesy of Doe Run Valley Books)

CRANBERRY FLUMMERY

Before the Civil War, flummeries were quite popular as breakfast and supper foods, especially for children, or following dinner as a dessert. Cornstarch pudding and tapioca eventually pushed flummery off the Victorian menu, yet this old-fashioned treat is well worth reviving.

The word *flummery* comes from the Welsh word *llymru*.[18] In Wales, it was a sour dish generally made with oatmeal and buttermilk, but in America, by the middle of the eighteenth century, rice became the primary cereal ingredient. Recipe variations were many, yet the basic concept was the same: a starchy pudding usually flavored and colored with fruit.[19] Red flummeries, to which red currant or cherry juice was added, were considered by many cooks to be the most festive, with cranberry flummery most often associated with Christmas. If it is made thick enough, flummery will set stiff and thus can be chilled in china or special wooden molds, which further enhances its festive appearance.

YIELD: 1 QUART, ENOUGH FOR 4 TO 6 SERVINGS.

¾ cup rice
4 cups fresh cranberries
1¾ cups sugar

2 tablespoons lemon juice
¼ teaspoon grated nutmeg
Milk (optional)

Put the rice in a blender or processor and pulse until the rice is broken down to a coarse cornmeal consistency. (The old method was to pound it in a mortar.) Put the rice meal into a heavy saucepan. Bring 2½ cups of water to a boil, pour it over the rice, and stir well. Cover and let stand at least 1 hour, but preferably overnight. In the morning, bring the mixture to a gentle boil. Once it boils, reduce the heat and simmer until it becomes thick and glutinous (about 15 to 20 minutes). Whisk often to reduce lumps and to maintain a creamy consistency.

While the rice is cooking, put the cranberries, sugar, lemon juice, and ¼ cup of water in a saucepan and cook until the berries begin to burst (about 10 minutes). Add the nutmeg. Pour into a blender or food processor and add the cooked rice. Purée until absolutely smooth and free of small lumps of rice. Pour into a china serving dish and put aside in the refrigerator to cool and set.

If you choose to use a china or wooden mold, first brush it lightly with milk before filling it with the flummery. Turn out of the mold right before serving. If you lack molds, simply use what most country people used anyway: a deep bowl or teacups.

Hand-thrown yellowware flummery bowl, northern New Jersey, circa 1810. Hot flummery was poured into these bowls to congeal.

FLUMMERY SAUCE

*F*lummery was usually served in a soup plate with cream and sugar, but you may also serve it with a cranberry sauce. The sauce below is a variation of an 1848 recipe for cranberry pie.

YIELD: 1 PINT.

4 cups fresh cranberries
¾ cup brown sugar
Juice of ½ lemon
Juice of ½ orange
Grated zest of 1 orange

*C*ombine all the ingredients in a saucepan and cook gently until the berries begin to burst (about 10 minutes). Serve cold as a sauce over the flummery. This sauce can also be served with roast duck, roast turkey, or venison.

SOURCE: Frances Harriet McDougall, *The Housekeeper's Book* (Philadelphia: William Marshall & Co., 1838), 159.

BROWN BETTY

YIELD: 4 TO 6 SERVINGS.

2½ pounds tart apples (about 6 large apples)
½ cup brown sugar
1 cup bread crumbs

4 tablespoons unsalted butter
½ cup apple cider

Preheat the oven to 350°F. Grease a baking dish, 3 inches deep, 8 inches in diameter.

Pare, core, and slice the apples and cover the bottom of the baking dish with them. Sprinkle with sugar, bread crumbs, and small bits of butter. Repeat with another layer of apples and continue in this order until the dish is full. The top layer should consist of bread crumbs. Dot with remaining bits of butter and pour the cider over it in a zigzag pattern so that the moisture will be evenly distributed. Bake uncovered for 1 hour. Serve hot or cold.

SOURCE: Eliza Leslie, *Miss Leslie's New Cookery Book* (Philadelphia: T. B. Peterson, 1857), 455.

Bringing in Christmas. Chromolithograph Christmas card, American, circa 1880. (Roughwood Collection)

A Christmas Greeting with love.

TWELFTH NIGHT CAKE
1807

If you intend to serve this on Twelfth Night, make the cake no later than November 30. I make mine on October 1.

YIELD: ONE 3½-POUND CAKE; APPROXIMATELY 15 TO 20 SERVINGS.

3 tablespoons coarsely chopped candied lemon peel
3 tablespoons coarsely chopped candied orange peel
¼ cup diced citron
2½ cups currants
4 tablespoons chopped blanched almonds
8 tablespoons amaretto

8 eggs
1 cup sugar
½ pound (2 sticks) unsalted butter
2¼ cups all-purpose flour
1 tablespoon ground cinnamon
1 tablespoon ground mace
1 large bean and 1 dried pea (optional)

Chop the lemon and orange peel and citron together until the mixture has the texture of rice. Mix with the currants and chopped almonds. Add the amaretto, cover, and infuse overnight. The next day, when you are ready to bake, preheat the oven to 275°F.

Beat the eggs and sugar until *very light*—this is important for the texture of the cake. Cream the butter and combine with the egg mixture. Sift the flour, cinnamon, and mace together twice, then sift it into the eggs, folding in a little at a time in order to keep the batter light. Then fold in the fruit and any unabsorbed liquid. Add a large bean and a pea if desired.

Grease a 9-inch tube pan, and line the bottom with baking parchment. Fill with batter and bake in the preheated oven for 2 hours. Cool the cake for about 20 minutes on a rack before removing it from the pan.

When the cake is cool, wrap it in cheesecloth dipped in brandy and store in an airtight container in a cool place for at least 1

Mold for paste sugar decorations for Twelfth Night Cake, circa 1845.
(Courtesy of the Castle Museum, York, England)

month before serving. Or follow the instructions for storing fruitcake in champagne on
page 93.

NOTE: I prefer to serve this cake uniced, but in former times, it was customary to coat the cake with
marzipan and then ice it with a royal icing. The
icing was usually ornamental, done up in swags and
flowers, much like our contemporary wedding
cakes. Figures of paste sugar were also added to the
top. In chapter 7 there are recipes for both marzipan
and paste sugar.

SOURCE: Frederic Nutt, *The Complete Confectioner*
(New York: Richard Scott, 1807), 29.

FRIED PIES

1914

In an article called "Christmas Cates" in *Good Housekeeping* for December 1914, Martha McCulloch-Williams launched into a long and detailed disquisition on Fried Pies, also known as Christmas Pasties. This is the same author who only the year before had published her popular *Dishes & Beverages of the Old South,* a book rich in details about Christmas.

The suggested filling for the pasties was dried fruit, preferably dried peaches, one of the most favored of all early American dried fruits. But since dried apples are now easier to obtain (and less likely to be processed with sugar), I have rearranged the recipe using apples instead. I have also taken into account her advice that dried apples demand allspice and cinnamon. As for peaches, if you use them, a "mere zest of cloves" (to use her expression) will do.

After all this fussing about spices, I should add that Miss Martha completely left out any hints about the right sort of dough for her pasties—pretty fundamental if you ask me. I have therefore dipped into Marion Harland's *Breakfast, Luncheon and Tea* for the solution.

YIELD: 4 TO 6 SERVINGS.

¼ pound dried apple slices
1 cup brown sugar
¼ teaspoon ground allspice
1 teaspoon ground cinnamon
½ cup currants (optional)
5 eggs, separated
½ cup confectioners' sugar

½ cup heavy cream
¼ teaspoon salt
1 teaspoon grated nutmeg
Grated zest of ½ lemon
2½ cups all-purpose flour
Lard or vegetable oil

Bring 2 cups water to a boil, pour over the apples, cover, and let stand overnight. In the morning, add the sugar and 1 cup water, and stew, uncovered, until the fruit is soft and the liquid has cooked out. Add the spices and purée to a thick pulp. Add the currants.

Beat the 5 yolks until light, then cream them with the sugar. Add the ½ cup of cream and beat until light. Beat the egg whites in a separate bowl until stiff; fold them into the yolk mixture with the salt, nutmeg, and lemon zest.

Sift in 2 cups of flour and gently work into a soft dough, using only as much of the remaining ½ cup of flour as necessary to keep the dough from sticking to the fingers. Dust the work surface with flour and roll out the dough about ½ inch thick, passing the rolling pin over it only once or twice. Excessive roll-ing will toughen the dough.

Heat the lard or vegetable oil in a deep fryer to 375°F. While the fat is heating, fill the pasties by cutting out rounds of dough 6 or 8 inches across and spreading *half* of each round with the fruit purée. Leave a small margin of dough around the edge. Fold over the uncovered half to form a pocket and press together along the edge. Fry a few at a time in the fat, drain, and serve warm, when they are at their best.

NOTE: If you want to serve these for dessert, you can make them up shortly ahead and keep them warm in a low oven. Or you can serve them cold stacked on a platter and dusted with superfine sugar. Children seem to like them either way.

SOURCES: Martha McCulloch-Williams, "Christmas Cates," *Good Housekeeping* (December 1914), 763. Marion Harland, *Breakfast, Luncheon and Tea* (New York: Scribner, Armstrong & Company, 1875), 287.

Gingerbread cannoneer from a wooden mold, circa 1815.

Wafer iron for Christmas wafers from the Werle Iron Foundry,
Ottweiler (Saarland), Germany, 1840–1870. A popular
exportware to the German community in America.

TWELFTH NIGHT WAFERS

1911

This is the recipe of Hattie King Taylor of Bristol, Tennessee, a region known more for its poverty than for recipes as rich as this one. I would describe these very decadent cookies as a cross between Italian *pasta frolla* and a sand tart.

YIELD: APPROXIMATELY 12 DOZEN 2-INCH COOKIES.

1 pound (4 sticks) unsalted butter
3¾ cups confectioners' sugar
6½ cups pastry flour
Yolks of 9 hard-boiled eggs
Grated zest of 1 lemon
2 tablespoons whiskey
Almonds or raisins for garnish
(optional)

The butter must be very cold. Chop it into pea-size bits and put into a large sieve. Set over a bowl. Add the sugar and 5 cups of flour, and rub to form a soft, sticky crumb. Grate the egg yolks and work them into the crumb with the grated lemon. Add the whiskey and work the dough with your fingers until it is completely smooth. Then add the remaining 1½ cups of flour and knead until the dough is no longer tacky. Form into a ball, cover, and store in the refrigerator to ripen overnight. The dough must be very cold when you work with it, so only break off what is needed at a time.

Preheat the oven to 325°F.

Dust your work surface with flour and roll out the dough ¼ inch thick. Cut into 2-inch rounds and set these on greased baking sheets. Bake 10-12 minutes, or until golden brown around the edges. Cool on racks.

NOTE: Mrs. Taylor suggested garnishing each cookie with a raisin or almond before baking. This increases their decorative appearance, but since the cookies are very rich to begin with, I hardly think this is necessary.

SOURCE: Mrs. Samuel Beckett Boyd, *The Tennessee and Virginia Cook Book* (Knoxville, Tenn.: First Presbyterian Church of Knoxville, 1911), 61.

WAFERS AND JELLY

1854

This recipe makes a delicate wafer reminiscent of old-fashioned ice cream cones. Served with fruit jellies or jam, the stack of wafers made an appealing and highly decorative sideboard dish for Christmas and New Years buffets, as shown on page 27.

YIELD: APPROXIMATELY 15 WAFERS, OR 12 SERVINGS WHEN ASSEMBLED INTO 3 LAYERED STACKS.

3 egg yolks
1½ cups superfine sugar
6 tablespoons unsalted butter, melted
2¾ cups all-purpose flour
½ cup water or rosewater

Fruit jelly or jam
Whipped cream
Crystallized flowers and candied angelica for garnish (optional)

Cream the eggs and sugar. Add the melted butter and beat until smooth. Gradually sift in the flour, a little at a time, alternating with 2 tablespoons of water or rosewater. This will form a soft dough.

Refer to my instructions for preparing a wafer iron for baking on page 73. Heat the wafer or pizzelle iron on both sides. Open it and grease it. The grease should sizzle and smoke. Place a ball of dough about the size of a large walnut in the middle of one of the sides of the iron. Keep it level, clamp it shut, and bake evenly on both sides. Allow about 3 minutes for each side. Or follow the instuctions that came with your pizzelle iron. When the wafers are done, cool them flat on racks.

Take 5 wafers and cover 4 of them with stiff fruit jelly or jam. Stack them on a plate and put the fifth wafer on top. Cut the stack into quarters. Garnish with whipped cream, and, if you like, add crystallized flowers and candied angelica.

NOTE: This dough may be frozen for later use. Unsaid but implied in the original recipe is that one should be using a wafer iron that is divided into quarters, as in a pattern with 4 hearts, or a rectangle divided into 4 sections. This makes the wafers easier to break into neat pieces.

SOURCE: *Arts Revealed, and Universal Guide* (New York: American Family Publication Establishment, 1854), 133.

Myrtle oranges and ground pines decorate a dessert table from the mid-nineteenth century. On the left, "Blozges" made with Amelia Simmons's Pound Cake (PAGE 87) after 1848 pastry book designs by Christian Neunhöfer. On the right, Wafers and Jelly and gilded New Years Cakes.

ORANGE FRITTERS

— 1809 —

*L*ike *Olie-koecken,* this is another fritter recipe that was especially popular at Christmas and New Years. The original recipe went to great lengths to remove bitter peels and to poach the fruit whole, which suggests to me that something akin to sour Seville oranges were being used. I recommend instead fresh blood oranges, tangerines, or mandarin oranges, since their size is small and closer to those used in the original. Also, the flavor of these oranges holds up better under deep-frying than the rather bland oranges sold in most supermarkets.

YIELD: 2 DOZEN FRITTERS.

6 oranges, mandarin or tangerine size
1 cup all-purpose flour
1 cup dry white wine
2 tablespoons unsalted butter, melted
Superfine sugar
Lard or vegetable oil

*P*eel the oranges and cut into quarters. Pick out the seeds. Sift the flour into the wine and beat to a ropy consistency. Then add the butter and beat smooth. While you are making the batter, heat the lard or vegetable oil in a deep fryer to 375°F and turn on the broiler in the oven.

Using a skewer or long-handled fork, such as a fondue fork, dip an orange quarter in the batter and slip it gently into the hot fat. Do this with a rolling action of the wrist in order to keep the batter as even as possible around the orange. Fry until golden brown, then drain. While still hot, roll the fritters in superfine sugar, then set them under the broiler only long enough to caramelize the sugar. Serve immediately.

NOTE: The tartness of the oranges is a perfect contrast to the crunchy caramel sweetness of the fritter coating. Before the days of oven broilers, caramelizing was achieved with a salamander, the implement illustrated below. The round end was stuck into a fire until it turned red hot. It was then passed over the sugar, with immediate results.

SOURCE: *Chester and Delaware Federalist* (West Chester, Pa.), 13 December, 1809.

Iron salamander, early nineteenth century.

ELLEN'S CRULLERS
1868

Crullers for most American cooks were irregular shapes of dough deep-fried in lard. Some people cut them in diamonds or strips, or even animal shapes. Several of the oldest medieval recipes for crullers flavored them with saffron.

Americans borrowed the term *cruller* from the Lower Rhineland, where it is used both by the Dutch and Germans but with many different localized meanings. In general, *krullen* meant *rolled,* but the manner of rolling varied from place to place, and this in turn affected the final shape of the crullers. Crullers could even be wafers rolled into tubes, as in the recipe for *Oblatgebackenes* on pages 65–66. Or, as in the 1553 recipe of Anna Welser of Augsburg, they could be strips of dough gathered together in a ball and deep-fried. She rolled them in confectioners' sugar and called them *Schnee-Ballen* or snow balls.[20] All of these things are crullers. Several traditional shapes are illustrated on page 63.

YIELD: 6 TO 8 SERVINGS.

5 eggs
½ cup sugar
¼ cup unsalted butter, melted
2 teaspoons grated nutmeg

2 cups all-purpose flour
Lard or vegetable oil
Confectioners' sugar
Powdered cinnamon

Beat the eggs to a thick, light cream, then add the sugar and beat until combined. Gradually add the melted butter, stirring as you proceed. Add the nutmeg. Sift in the flour, sifting and stirring until a soft dough forms. Dust your fingers with flour and knead the dough gently for 2 or 3 minutes. Dust your work surface with flour and roll out the dough to a thickness of about ¼ inch. Cut into strips, animals, or irregular shapes with a jagging iron.

While you are cutting out the crullers, heat the lard or vegetable oil in a deep-fryer or deep cooking pot until it reaches 375°F. Drop in no more than 8 crullers at a time if you are using a small home fryer. Fry until golden brown, lift from the fat, drain, and dust liberally with confectioners' sugar mixed with cinnamon. These are best served the day they are made.

SOURCE: *Mrs. Winslow's Domestic Receipt Book for 1869* (New York: Jeremiah Curtis & Son and John I. Brown & Sons, 1868), 15.

TWO

Humbug Pie

HOW THE POOR BROUGHT IN CHRISTMAS

*I*t is easy enough today to look back on the Twelfth Night balls, the Christmas mumming, the great fruitcakes, the pies stuffed with game and other culinary tours de force and forget that this was not the Christmas savored by all. In England, in the old days of communal feasting, there was a certain seasonal leveling out of riches: the better-off in the village saw to it that the neediest were helped, and it was not unusual for widows or the elderly to carry off second or third helpings from the manor table to tide themselves over the holiday season.

No such comparable system existed in America, except in the South, where slaves developed their own counterpart to the serf's Saturnalia. For the slave, Christmas heralded not only feasting and revelry, but a period of freedom when the burdens of endless labor could be forgotten or at least set aside for the duration of the last week of the year. In essence, Christmas meant vacation. For this reason, blacks called it *Jubilee.*

Documentation of the Afro-American Christmas before the Civil War is not common, at least that part of it celebrated out of sight of white observers. Yet the following account from Jackson, Mississippi, in 1844 should throw some light on the general for-

New Orleans Gingerbread garnished with hickory nuts (TOP LEFT); Ideal Cookies spilling from an Afro-American coil basket (CENTER RIGHT); and at the bottom, Sweet Johnny Cake ornamented with popcorn "grannies" (unpopped kernels) and stamped with the handle of an old tin cup. On the bottom right, dried peaches, dried cherries, and tomato figs.

mat of the holiday as Afro-Americans experienced it.

On arriving at Jackson, during the day, I found the town almost literally filled with colored people, of both sexes, some dancing, some singing, and some fiddling, and all showing greater indications of freedom than, as it seemed to me, was desireable. By a sort of common law, in this country, in which the slaves are full as well as instructed as their masters, the time from Christmas to New Year is set apart as holidays, and all labor upon the plantation ceases. The privilege is enjoyed by most of the slaves, as an incident to the occasion, to carry to market on Christmas day such articles as they had raised upon a patch of ground assigned to them, or obtained by their labor during such leisure periods as have been given them as a reward for faithful service. Negroes from the distance of

Baking scene in rural Virginia.

The Christmas Cook

many miles around were seen coming into town, and during the whole day, some on horseback, some riding mules, some in wagons, some in ox-carts, and some on foot, with their various articles of produce for sale. Some had rice, some had eggs, some had chickens, some had baskets and brooms, some had bags of corn, some had various articles of mechanical skill, some had specimens of needlework, such as collars, pincushions, needle cases, etc., made by the females, some had loads of coarse grass, cut on the marches, and cured as hay, and some had nothing at all.[1]

The photograph on page 30 shows a number of nineteenth-century objects made by Southern blacks for similar Christmas markets. The small objects, not surprisingly, were sold to children, while the coil baskets were used for food storage.[2] Other items associated with Christmas, at least among Maryland blacks, were bottle gourds painted with African motifs and used as rattles during Christmas revelry.[3]

On plantations where liberal management was practiced, each slave household might receive a shoulder of bacon, a turkey, a goose, and a barrel of cider at Christmas.[4] Such generosity was certainly cause for happy feasting. Yet in terms of general menu, especially so far as dessert foods were concerned, perhaps the Sweet Johnny Cake, with its added ingredients of sugar, eggs, and nutmeg, best represents the level of luxury that most plantation slaves savored during the yuletide season.

Sweet Johnny Cake, a species of cornmeal gingerbread baked as a flat cake, is probably also one of the oldest forms of Christmas food in the South. It is based on the bannock of the British Isles, a cake that traces into Celtic antiquity. Being a flat cake molded with the hands, the Johnny Cake could be baked on a board by any open fire. Furthermore, the simple ingredients were available to everyone—a cook could even substitute wild honey for the sugar.

Poor whites also made Sweet Johnny Cakes, although the only authentic recipe that I have thus far located—and published in this book—came from a black cook in Maryland. This old festive cake gradually fell out of fashion once chemical leaveners came on the scene in the 1830s and 1840s because cooks could then create lighter and more succulent cakes. New Orleans Gingerbread, which is truly half corn bread and half raised cake, is an example of this kind of transformation. Many black and poor white families in the South have preserved heirloom recipes like this as parts of their Christmas heritage.

As for working-class Americans in general, the elegant *ambigues* of Miss Hoofnagle's Twelfth Night ball were well beyond the reach of most Christmas cooks, yet they were ever adept at creating their own clever substitutes. Ice cream, which was a luxury food in the early nineteenth century, could be manufactured very easily with a large bowl of fresh fallen snow. Elizabeth Ellicott Lea published directions for doing just this

Humbug Pie: How the Poor Brought in Christmas

in her *Domestic Cookery,* and I have included her recipe at the end of this chapter. It is delightful!

Fig pie was another luxury dessert in early America. Dried figs generally came from Spain or Italy and were therefore far too expensive for most households. Tomato figs supplied an ingenious alternative.

Tomato figs, which came into vogue about 1845, could be chopped up and baked in pies in the manner of true figs.[5] To make the figs, plum tomatoes were poached whole in a syrup of brown sugar, then sun dried. Externally, they do resemble dried figs, but they retain a distinct tomato character. In fig pie, they remind me of green tomato mincemeat, yet another economy dish for Christmas.

Ersatz mincemeat was also made with chopped lemons, as in the case of Methodist Mincemeat, or with raisins and rolled crack-

Backyard fireworks kept Christmas Day jumping throughout the South. From an 1870 wood engraving.
(Roughwood Collection)

The Christmas Cook

ers, as in New England Humbug Pie. This dish doubtless owes its name to Scrooge in Dickens's *A Christmas Carol,* but with certain allusion to the begrudging acceptance of Christmas by old-line New Englanders after the Civil War. Like Methodist Mincemeat, it is an avowed temperance recipe, for which reason its other spiritual shortcomings were generally forgiven, well, sometimes.

Today we have forgotten the relentless attacks the temperance movement unleashed against Christmas in the nineteenth century and the strange side effects this had on cookery. Apropos Humbug Pie, I am reminded of John Staily, keeper of the Liverpool Inn in Perry County, Pennsylvania. In 1866, he experienced a change of heart about drink and tavern keeping, and without telling his family, praised the Lord, closed the barroom, and emptied out all the liquor on the floor. When his wife came in to get some whiskey for her baking, she was aghast, not so much at the sudden conversion, but that "he should at least have spared her some liquor for the mince pies."[6] In the eyes of Christmas cooks like Mrs. Staily, Humbug Pie could not have been more deservingly named.

American preachers were ever vigilant to remind their flocks about the pitfalls of drink and overfeasting. A visitation with this message in mind was something that could be expected during the holiday season. Poor cooks were often hard pressed to come up with suitable dishes, which as a matter of family pride and out of respect for their guest, had to represent the best they could

offer. This gave rise to a broad variety of folk names for foods made only when the preacher came calling.

For example, we find it in the Lower Virginia expression "gospel birds" for chickens served to the preacher for dinner.[7] Gospel birds were often earmarked as such while in the yard and kept alive against the time when the preacher should appear. In the meantime, they laid eggs that could be sold for cash or used up with great lavishness in a festive dessert called Preacher Pie. There is a recipe for that at the end of this chapter.

Country folk certainly would have been shocked at the expense of the New Years Pie discussed earlier and many of the other fancy Christmas dishes served by city dwellers. For farmers, Christmas was a time to collect profits, not to squander them.

John Janney, who lived in Fairfax County, Virginia, recalled that in the 1820s his family often fattened up geese and hogs to send to Christmas market in Alexandria, but at home "a fat goose on the table was not very common."[8] When we read in the diary of Martha Ogle Forman that on December 19, 1839, she killed two geese and four ducks and hung them in the garret (to age in the cold until the twenty-fifth), we are previewing dinner preparations for a wealthy plantation in Delaware, not that of the average farmer.[9]

If country folk were lucky enough to bag a wild turkey, so much the better for that meat was free. Yet many poor folk chose to settle for small game, and that often meant on Christmas Day a roast groundhog instead of suckling pig, some wild ducks, a songbird pie, or stewed squirrels. Instead of boiled plum pudding, they might have Suet Pudding, which is still popular as a Christmas dish in parts of the Midwest. Or they might eat American Plum Pudding made with crackers and inexpensive dried fruit, such as cherries, wild plums, and peaches. They would have blackberry preserves made with brown sugar and pies with dried elderberries instead of raisins. With dinner, they would drink elderberry wine instead of port and cherry wine instead of claret. For dessert, they might serve Brown Betty since apples were cheap, or apple fritters; instead of a plum cake, they might dish up Hard Times Fruitcake made with dried apples and much like dark chocolate when aged to perfection.

If, on the other hand, they were Germans living in Pennsylvania, Maryland, Ohio, or northern Virginia, they might very well set up a Christmas tree and lavish some of the profits from Christmas market on marzipans and clear toys and other confections available from the shops in town. For the Germans in America, Christmas belonged to the children. And so far as the children were concerned, it was not Christmas without a tree.

Cup Cake, or Poor Man's Pound Cake
1837

In the manuscript cookbook of Josephine Lammott Smith of Union Bridge, Carroll County, Maryland, this recipe is called Poor Man's Pound Cake, one of several folk names.[10] She made it with leftover bread dough to which sugar and other ingredients were added. Most of these rural adaptations can be traced to a master recipe that appeared in 1837 in Caroline Gilman's *Lady's Annual Register,* one of the most popular Christmas gift books that season. Gilman's comment about the recipe explained its approval among country cooks: "As good as pound cake, but cheaper."

The original cakes were baked in small tin or earthenware cups, or in homes where even these were lacking, in an array of old teacups.

YIELD: 24 SERVINGS.

½ pound (2 sticks) unsalted butter
2 cups sugar
4 eggs

4 tablespoons rosewater
1½ teaspoons grated nutmeg
1½ cups all-purpose flour

Preheat the oven to 375°F. Grease 2 cupcake pans, 12 cups to a pan.

Cream the butter and sugar until light. Beat the eggs to a froth, then combine with the butter mixture. Add the rosewater and nutmeg. Sift in the flour and gradually work into a thick batter. Fill each cupcake cup with approximately ¼ cup of batter. Bake in the preheated oven for 20 minutes.

NOTE: It is advisable to remove the cupcakes from the pans while they are still warm. Once they cool, they tend to stick to the pans. This problem can be avoided by using paper liners in the cupcake pans.

SOURCE: Caroline Gilman, *Lady's Annual Register and Housewife's Memorandum-Book for 1838* (Boston: T. H. Carter, 1837), 96.

Tin baking cups for Poor Man's Pound Cake, circa 1860.

Humbug Pie: How the Poor Brought in Christmas

Chromolithograph trade cards, circa 1885.

Compliments of A MERRY CHRISTMAS.
ISAAC W. KEIM,
Wholesale Dealer in WINES & LIQUORS,
S. E. Cor. 6th & Washington Sts., Reading Pa.

HARD TIMES FRUITCAKE

1865

*I*n company with Poor Man's Pound Cake and Hard Times Molasses Cake, this emergency recipe gained widespread circulation in the North following the Civil War—emergency in that it makes do with cheap, local ingredients during times of shortage.

The recipe originated in South Carolina about 1862 under the name of Confederate Plum Cake. There are several versions of it. Most of the wartime Confederate versions were made with sorghum syrup instead of molasses and various mixtures of cheap dried fruit. Dried cherries, for example, usually took the place of raisins, and weak lye took the place of commercial baking powders. Carolinians often flavored the recipe with the powdered dried rind of a local bush orange called the myrtle-leaved orange (citrus myrtifolia) pictured on page 43.

YIELD: TWO 8-INCH LOAVES, APPROXIMATELY 10 TO 15 SERVINGS.

2 cups chopped dried apples	1 teaspoon baking soda
2¼ cups molasses	2 teaspoons ground cinnamon
12 tablespoons butter	1 teaspoon ground cloves
1 egg	1 teaspoon ground allspice
2 cups all-purpose flour	

*P*ut the chopped apples in a deep bowl and pour over 3 cups of boiling water. Cover and let stand overnight. The next day, drain and press out any excess liquid. Put the fruit in a saucepan with 1 cup of molasses and cook until the fruit begins to turn dark brown and most of the liquid is absorbed (about 40 minutes). Put the fruit in a colander to drain.

Preheat the oven to 275°F. Grease two 8-inch loaf pans.

Cream the butter, then beat in the remaining 1¼ cups molasses. Beat the egg to a froth and fold into the batter. Sift the flour, soda, and spices twice, then sift into the batter. Fold in the fruit and pour the batter into the pans. Bake for 1½ hours, or until the cakes test done in the middle. Cool 20 minutes on a rack before removing from the pans.

NOTE: Having made this several times, I can only describe it as an unusual species of moist ginger-

bread that looks and tastes something like dark chocolate cake, but is totally uninteresting until it is sufficiently aged. To age, wrap the cakes in cheesecloth dipped in applejack and store 6 months in an airtight container in a cool place, such as an unheated room. The aging process can be accelerated by freezing. Freeze the cakes 3 weeks, then thaw and serve. The special flavor imparted by the applejack will not be present, which is a pity. Brushing the cakes with applejack after they thaw will not fool the cognoscenti.

SOURCE: *The Agricultural Almanac for 1866* (Lancaster, Pa.: Printed by John Baer, 1865), unpaginated.

Humbug Pie: How the Poor Brought in Christmas

METHODIST MINCEMEAT

—— 1827 ——

*T*his recipe was originally intended for small pies baked in pattypans, but it also works well in large pies intended as table centerpieces. With that in mind, I have provided some recipes for pie crusts in chapter 4. You might want to try one of them for this recipe—Susannah Carter's crust for pattypans is excellent.

YIELD: SIX 4½- TO 5-INCH DOUBLE-CRUST PIES.

Short crust
1 large lemon
8 tablespoons (1 stick) unsalted butter
½ cup brown sugar
1½ cups currants
3 large apples
⅓ cup lemon juice
2 teaspoons ground cinnamon
¼ teaspoon ground cloves
1 teaspoon grated nutmeg
½ cup chopped citron

*L*ine six 4½- to 5-inch pie pans or 12 tartlet pans with short crust. Remove the pithy membranes from the lemon and cut the rind into quarters. Place the rind in a saucepan and cover with boiling water. Simmer 20 to 30 minutes, or until the rind is tender. Strain, reserve the lemon rind, and discard the bitter water. Chop the rind very fine in a food processor.

Preheat the oven to 350°F.

Melt the butter in a deep stewing pan, add the sugar and currants and cover. Stew the currants until they are plumped. Pare, core, and chop the apples, and add them to the currants together with the chopped lemon rind, the lemon juice, and the spices. Cook for 15 minutes, then add the citron and remove from the stove.

When the filling is cool enough to work with, fill the pie shells and cover them with a top crust. Bake the 4½- to 5-inch pies in the preheated oven for approximately 25 to 30 minutes; the tartlets will bake in about 20 minutes.

NOTE: If you are not a Methodist, you may add 2 tablespoons of lemon cordial or brandy to the filling before you fill the pies. After all, the alcohol bakes out.

SOURCE: The Christian Advocate and Journal (New York), 16 November 1827.

Hard Times Fruit Cake garnished with dried fruit (TOP LEFT), Peanut Macaroons, Poor Man's Pound Cake iced in the style of the 1820s, Shellbark Cakes (FAR LEFT), and a large pie of Methodist Mincemeat furnish a working man's version of Christmas luxury.

HUMBUG PIE

1874

There is a variation of this called Turn-Under Pie. After the pie is baked, the top crust is removed whole, turned over like a shallow dish and set on a platter. The contents of the pie are then poured over the crust. This serving technique is very old among Anglo-Americans, and continued to be a prevalent habit in rural households where members of the family ate from a common dish placed in the middle of the table.

YIELD: APPROXIMATELY 8 SERVINGS.

Short crust
1 cup molasses
1 cup brown sugar
1 cup chopped raisins
1 cup cracker crumbs (see note)
1 cup cold water
½ cup vinegar

2 tablespoons butter, melted
1¼ teaspoons ground mace
1 teaspoon ground allspice
1 teaspoon ground cinnamon
1 teaspoon salt
Cold water and granulated sugar

Preheat the oven to 400°F.

Line a 9- or 10-inch pie plate with short crust. Mix all of the ingredients in a large bowl. Let this stand for about 10 minutes so that the cracker crumbs are thoroughly soaked. Fill the pie shell and cover with a top crust. Decorate the crust with pastry figures, brush it lightly with cold water, and sprinkle granulated sugar over it. Bake for 10 minutes at 400°F, then reduce the heat to 350°F and bake for 30 to 35 minutes, or until the center is set. Serve hot or cold.

NOTE: It is important that your cracker crumbs be very fine. If they are coarse, spread them on a work table and roll them with a rolling pin or pound them in a mortar. If the crumbs are too coarse, the pie will not thicken. As a precaution, you may add about 1 tablespoon cornstarch or potato flour to the crumbs before they are mixed with the filling.

SOURCE: *The Household* (Brattleboro, Vt.) 7 (November 1874), 255.

NEW ORLEANS GINGERBREAD

1856

Hannah Hungary Widdifield (1768–1854) was a Quaker confectioner in Philadelphia and rival of Elizabeth Goodfellow. Like Mrs. Goodfellow, she also ran a cooking school, and her recipes are structured after the Goodfellow method, that is, ingredients are listed first.

In this, one of Widdifield's most charming Christmas recipes, grated orange zest adds unusual character to the flavor.

YIELD: 8 TO 12 SERVINGS.

½ pound (2 sticks) unsalted butter
½ cup brown sugar
Grated zest of 1 orange
1¾ cups all-purpose flour
1 tablespoon ground ginger
1 teaspoon ground cinnamon
1 tablespoon baking soda
2 cups fine white cornmeal, less
2½ tablespoons
6 eggs
1½ cups unsulfured molasses
¼ cup milk

Preheat the oven to 350°F.

Cream the butter and sugar with the orange zest until light. Sift together the flour, ginger, cinnamon, and baking soda twice, then combine with the cornmeal.

Beat the eggs to a thick froth; combine with the molasses and milk. Add the egg mixture to the butter mixture, then gradually sift in the dry ingredients. Take care as you sift and fold in the dry ingredients that you keep the batter as light as possible.

Grease a rectangular or round baking pan and line the bottom with greased baking parchment. About pan size, I would suggest something measuring 8½ by 14 by 2 inches. (You may also use 2 twelve-cup muffin pans, allowing 20 to 25 minutes baking time.) Spread the batter evenly over the bottom and smooth the surface with a knife. Bake 35 to 40 minutes. Serve hot or cold.

NOTE: Do not forget to remove 2½ tablespoons of cornmeal from the 2 cups measured; this will compensate for the difference between old-style cornmeal and the commercial cornmeal of today.

SOURCE: Hannah Hungary Widdifield, *Widdifield's New Cook Book* (Philadelphia: T. B. Peterson and Brothers, 1856), 369.

PREACHER PIE

This is the recipe of Mrs. James A. Hensley of Knoxville, Tennessee.

YIELD: ONE 9- TO 10-INCH PIE (SERVES 8 PREACHERS).

6 tablespoons unsalted butter
¾ cup granulated sugar
4 eggs, separated
1 cup cream

⅓ cup chopped citron
⅓ cup chopped raisins
One 9- to 10-inch short crust pie shell
4 tablespoons superfine sugar

Preheat the oven to 325°F.

Cream the butter and sugar. Beat the yolks until thick, then combine with the butter mixture. Beat in the cream.

Scatter the chopped citron and raisins over the bottom of the pie shell and spread the batter over this evenly. Set the pie in the preheated oven and bake for 45 minutes, or until set in the center. Remove the pie from the oven and reset the temperature to 350°F.

Beat the egg whites to a stiff froth and add the superfine sugar. Spread the meringue over the top of the pie and brown in the oven for 10 minutes.

SOURCE: Mrs. Samuel Beckett Boyd, *The Tennessee and Virginia Cook Book* (Knoxville, Tenn.: privately printed, 1911), 174.

SNOW ICE CREAM

1853

Elizabeth Ellicott Lea would not have approved of the rum I have added to this recipe, but it makes the dish sinfully delicious.

1 cup heavy cream
¼ cup superfine sugar
2 teaspoons lemon extract, or 2 tablespoons rosewater (see note)

Mix the cream, sugar, and flavoring. Then add the snow—the precise amount will depend on the texture. Beat together with a spoon or whisk, adding only enough snow to make a stiff ice cream. Adjust sugar if necessary. Serve immediately.

Naturally, you must begin with clean, fresh-fallen snow.

YIELD: 8 SERVINGS.

8 to 10 cups fresh, fluffy snow

NOTE: Instead of lemon extract or rosewater, add 2 teaspoons vanilla extract and ¼ cup rum. Wonderful!

SOURCE: Elizabeth Ellicott Lea, *Domestic Cookery* (Baltimore: Cushings and Bailey, 1853), 111.

Humbug Pie: How the Poor Brought in Christmas

SWEET JOHNNY CAKE
1878

Philadelphia confectioner James Parkinson put out a call for Sweet Johnny Cake in 1878 in answer to a request for the rare recipe by one of the correspondents to *The Confectioners' Journal,* which he helped edit.[11] A black cook from Hagerstown, Maryland, identified only as "Sam," responded. This is Sam's recipe.

Having made it many times, I cannot imagine Sweet Johnny Cake baked anywhere but before an open fire. The flavor is unique, and I think the one-directional heat has much to do with the traditional, soft, crumbly texture. Johnny Cakes were baked on a wide board—oak or poplar are best— propped up before a brisk fire. The cakes were shaped by hand, and several little signs indicated when they were done: the way the dough pulled around the edges from the board, the color change, the smell of the baking cornmeal, the steam. It was an acquired instinct that did not come from cookbooks, and black cooks were the unchallenged masters of this art.

On the other hand, I am aware that many readers would rather try this in their oven. Therefore, I have provided procedures for preparing the dish both ways.

YIELD: TWO 7-INCH JOHNNY CAKES.

4 tablespoons unsalted butter
4 tablespoons brown sugar
3 eggs
1¼ cups all-purpose flour

1¼ cups white cornmeal
1½ teaspoons grated nutmeg
1 egg white
1 tablespoon water

Cream the butter and sugar. Beat the eggs to a froth and combine with the sugar mixture. Sift the flour, cornmeal, and grated nutmeg together, then sift this into the other ingredients. Work into a dough and knead on a lightly floured work surface. Knead until spongy, using only enough flour to keep the dough from being tacky.

Hearth method: Preheat your baking board before the fire. Break the dough into 2 equal balls and spread 1 of these on the hot baking board until it is about 7 inches in diameter. Pat it out so that it is thinner around the edges than in the middle. Score with a sharp knife. Beat the egg white and water to a froth and brush the cake with it.

Set the board before a brisk fire, tipping it up until it is almost perpendicular to the hearth. When the surface turns golden brown and the edges have pulled away from the board (in about 15 to 20 minutes), lift it carefully with a spatula, turn it over, and stand it against the board or on a rack with the unbaked side toward the fire. Brown this side, then serve hot. Split it open like a pita bread and put butter on the inside. Repeat as above with the other ball of dough.

Oven method: Preheat the oven to 375°F. Divide the dough into 2 equal balls. Put them on a greased baking sheet and pat out to form round cakes about 7 inches in diameter, thinner at the edges than in the middle. Score with a sharp knife and brush with the egg white and water beaten to a froth. Bake in the preheated oven 20 to 25 minutes, or until golden brown on top and the edges have lifted from the baking sheet. Turn the cakes over and brown the undersides for about 10

to 15 minutes. Serve immediately. Split them open like pita breads and put butter on the inside.

SOURCE: *The Confectioners' Journal* 3 (January 1878), 22.

Nineteenth-century engraving of a slave cook in Virginia

Martin Luther's Christmas Tree

Martin Luther never saw a Christmas tree even though he has been pictured often enough sitting in his stove room at Wittenberg with a *Tannenbaum* all aglow.[1] It is well-documented that whatever Christmas trees may have existed in Luther's era, they certainly were not looked upon with favor by the clergy—Protestant or Catholic.

In Germany, like England, the Christmas tree and the custom of decorating the house with evergreens were historically connected. The tree, however, was a recent outgrowth of an older, less formalized custom of bringing living greens into the home. The antecedents of this tradition are ancient and today the pre-Christian connections are a subject of heated controversy among cultural histo-

rians.[2] Our interest here is primarily in how this type of decoration encouraged Christmas cookery. Certainly, decorative impulses increase when attention is focused on a large bush in the center of the room. But beyond this, the coming of the Christmas tree heralded a major shift in Christmas entertaining. It marked a retreat from older forms of communal feasting to feasting at home. The family rather than the larger community be-

Christmas among the Pennsylvania Dutch. On the left, a *Grischdaagszweeg* or *Zuckerbaam* of wild cherry branches; on the pewter charger, a pyramid of apples and boxwood. In the basket on the left, various gingerbreads, Springerle cookies, and diamond-shaped Almond Cakes (PAGE 136); in the basket on the right, *Oblatgebackenes* (PAGE 65); and around the base of the pyramid, Sweet Pretzels (PAGE 126).

came the central theme of Christmas, with special emphasis on children.

In describing the German settlers of early Funkstown in western Maryland, Thomas Scharf noted: "They put themselves to a good deal of trouble and were quite lavish in their expenditures in providing Christmas trees for the amusement of the young folks, and upon these was hung almost every conceivable thing that could be made out of sugar that would please and gratify the youthful members of the family."[3] This fits the popular image of the old Pennsylvania and Maryland German Christmas. Yet in

This 1855 engraving is an American combination of two separate European prints: one depicting Luther and his family in a fictional setting at Wittenberg in 1536 by Carl A. Schwerdgeburth (1785–1878); the other, Hugo Bürkner's engraving of Christmas at Wandsbecker Schloss near Berlin in 1796.

The Christmas Cook

those parts of colonial America where many Germans settled in the early eighteenth century, a medley of Middle European Christmas customs was practiced. Sometimes these customs were grafted onto older Anglo-American traditions, in other cases, they were practiced side by side.[4]

Prior to the appearance of the evergreen Christmas tree in Pennsylvania in the late eighteenth century, there were earlier and historically much older types of "trees" brought into the house. Ultimately, this custom traces its roots to eastern Gaul (present-day eastern France and Germany west of the Rhine), where the worship of trees was practiced among the ancient Celtic peoples who lived there. Evergreens played a role in the Festival of Imbolic (February 1), a major turning point in the Celtic year. At this time mock wars between winter and summer took place. These mock battles were repeated at Beltane (May 1). German and French folk culture preserved many of these pagan rites by moving their observance to acceptable holidays on the Christian calendar. Over time, the original meanings were lost or intermingled with Christian practice. One of these was the *Grischdaagsmoije* of the Pennsylvania Dutch.

The *Grischdaagsmoije* (literally Christmas May Pole) or *Grischdaagszweeg* (Christmas Frond) might consist of a large limb of mountain laurel set in a tub on the table.[5] This greenery would be hung with such things as apples, pictorial wafers called *Oblaten* (see

E. FERRETT & CO.
PHILADELPHIA
1845.

Illustration from an 1845 children's book depicting a *Grischdaagsmoije* of mountain laurel. (Library of Congress)

the recipe for *Oblatgebackenes* on pages 65–66), ornamental honey cakes, and if the family were well-off, perhaps some sugar-work or marzipan purchased in a nearby town—certainly not so much candy as Scharf would have us believe. This pre-Christmas tree custom was particularly strong among the German settlers who came from Alsace and the Palatinate, more than 40 percent of the German-speaking population.[6]

Martin Luther's Christmas Tree

An alternate form of this tradition consisted of a large branch cut from a cherry tree and brought into the house on St. Barbara's Day (December 4) so that it would bloom by Christmas. This too might be decorated. The custom, very popular among the Swabian element, originated in connection with medieval observances of St. Barbara. In religious iconography, her symbol was a stone tower in reference to her martyrdom. But in folk art, her attribute was the cherry, which appears even today as a decorative motif on Springerle cookies. Candy and marzipan cherries hung on Christmas trees of the eighteenth and nineteenth centuries also alluded to this saint. An Ohio German recipe for cherries from beet preserves can be found in chapter 7.

In the 1740s, the Moravians from southeast Germany and Silesia (now in Poland) brought to Pennsylvania the custom of constructing Christmas pyramids. These were wooden tabletop structures built to carry evergreens, candles, and, invariably, apples that were usually set up in the place of worship as part of the Christmas Eve service. Sometimes the pyramids were additionally decorated with gingerbread and cookies, which were distributed to the children when the service was over.

The custom of making these pyramids originally developed in Saxony among the salt miners, who used their training in the construction of models of wooden mining structures—such as vertical windmills to ventilate the shafts—to make miniature me-chanical gadgets for their own pleasure.[7] Eventually, as mining declined, this craft developed into an active cottage industry of its own, and by the middle of the nineteenth century, Saxony became well-established as a center for all sorts of Christmas wares made of wood. It is interesting to note that the miners considered St. Barbara their patroness, thus her attributes appear as a motif in the Christmas folk art of this region as well.

It was in the Protestant areas of Germany where the Christmas tree custom as we now know it first took root. It was brought into general usage not through the churches, but through the Protestant guild halls, and from there the new fashion spread from town to town. For example, a *Dattelbäumchen* was recorded in a Bremen guild hall in 1570.[8] It was decorated with apples, nuts, dates (*Datteln*, hence the tree's name), pretzels, and paper flowers. The children shook it on Christmas Day to collect the goodies that fell off, a free-for-all to be sure! Shaking the tree on Christmas Day, or more commonly on Twelfth Night, was one of the oldest and most consistent customs associated with the Christmas tree. This custom was discarded only when candles came into use on the trees. In practice, the Christmas tree served as a secular replacement for Saint Nicholas and the Christ Child, who were the gift bringers at Christmas in the pre-Reformation period.

In the Protestant regions of the Rhineland, the Christmas tree also generally replaced the crêche as the focus of Christmas in the home. The Franciscan order introduced the crêche in the Middle Ages as part of the Cult of the Bambino Jesu. For many Protestants, the crêche, with its multitudes of wooden figures, represented a form of idolatry, a direct transfer of churchly images into the house. Today, it is not rare to see a crêche and a tree together, but in the first two centuries of its existence, the Christmas tree usually stood quite apart.

In the German-speaking parts of Alsace, where Christmas trees appeared in private homes by the early 1600s, the custom of cutting greens for Christmas was long associated with Adam and Eve Day (December 24), which not only equated evergreens with the Tree of Life, but provided a Christian explanation for an otherwise preexisting custom. The use of apples in connection with Christmas, the serpent as a decorative image on cookies, and the Adam and Eve motif in general all allude to this Christianizing influence.

On the other hand, church fathers were wary of the older pre-Christian connotations and went to great pains to contain the feasting within prescribed limits. Some ordinan-

Swiss and German cookies decorated with sugar icings that allude to or parody the Adam and Eve motif. On the right, a *Wickelkind* or Baby Cake.

Martin Luther's Christmas Tree

ces from as early as the 1400s specifically forbid the gathering of Christmas *Maien,* large evergreen branches cut to decorate both the stove room (the main heated room in a German house) and the stables. In more lenient areas of Alsace, such as Schlettstadt, ordinances permitted the cutting of *Maien,* so long as they did not exceed eight feet in length. The point here was that with the threshhold of sin at eight feet, it was not possible to erect tall poles.

The word *Maien,* the term used in the old ordinances, is not German; it is a French loan word, or more correctly, it stems from Gaulish, that semi-Latin language spoken by Continental Celts. In any case, the term means "maypole" and it is written in Pennsylvania-Dutch dialect as *Moije.* The primitive Christmas tree as a species of midwinter maypole may not be farfetched in terms of prevailing folk beliefs, but that is a large and highly complex study tangential to this book. I mention it only to suggest how far removed the tree originally may have been from a Christian connection. This is especially important to keep in mind when we come shortly to the High Church Movement.

The Christmas *Maien* survived in folk custom for many hundreds of years. One form of it was a bush or cluster of branches hung from the ceiling of a room. An illustration at right from J. P. Hebel's *Alemannische Gedichte* (Alemannic Poems) of 1806 shows a Christmas *Maien,* which he referred to in his book as a *Bäumli* (a "wee bough"). It is

A *Grischdaagsmoije* hanging from the ceiling of the *Kammer* or master bedroom of a German farmhouse. From Hebel's *Alemannische Gedichte* (1806). (Courtesy of the Van Pelt Library, University of Pennsylvania)

decorated with ribbons, fruit, and multitudes of human and animal figures in pastry. In the mother's lap is a small rye straw basket filled with cookies.

In the cookies we recognize many familiar pagan shapes: deer, horses, goats, roosters, geese, pigs, and most prominently, a man. All of these figural cookies appear as common ornaments on nineteenth-century American Christmas trees. Yet it is not likely that the pre-Christian themes represented in these motifs were understood by most Christmas cooks beyond the fact that they were simply old. More likely, these traditional images had been reassigned new meanings in line with Christian teachings, in short, a new label on an old bottle. This is especially common in early children's books intended as Christmas and New Years gifts.

In an 1837 gift book printed in Massachusetts called *The Twelve Months of the Year,* illustrated below, each month is assigned an animal or relevant scene and a moralizing story with a strong biblical theme. For December, the animal chosen is a ram, which happens to be the zodiac sign for the end of that month, hardly an early Christian image. Regardless, the woodcuts in this book served as models for a series of paste sugar molds made about the same time, one of which is shown beside the December ram. These sugar animals could be used as ornaments on

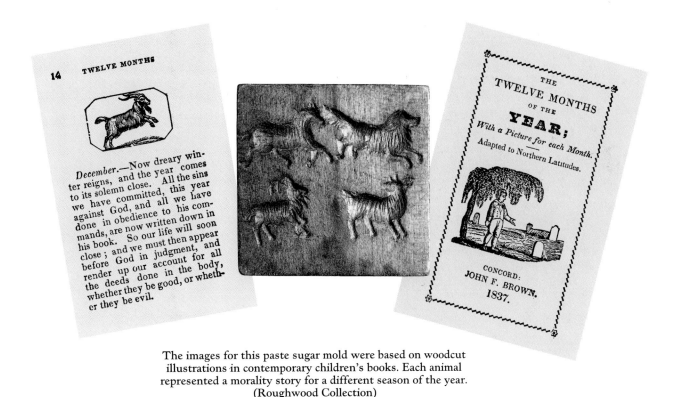

The images for this paste sugar mold were based on woodcut illustrations in contemporary children's books. Each animal represented a morality story for a different season of the year.
(Roughwood Collection)

larger iced cookies or on cakes, and doubtless the children were reminded of their moral significance, particularly if the cookies were distributed in the form of a reward.

Another example of this is in the representation of a man with a walking stick. In Twelfth Night masquerades, he was a standard character known by a variety of names such as Old Bachelor, Farmer Stump, and Peter Pippin. The Low Church denominations, among the Presbyterians and Methodists, who were opposed to such Twelfth Night frolicking, took the characters, and, like the zodiac ram, transformed them into little morality plays of their own. Thus, Old Bachelor became the Corrupt Man. His earthly corruption by wealth is detailed in a metamorphosis (folding picture book) for

The "Corrupt Man" as shown in an 1843 *Metamorphosis* (folding picture book). When the picture is lifted (CENTER), his earthly riches vanish as he changes into a skeleton. A Gingerbread mold (RIGHT) depicting the "Corrupt Man," circa 1830. (Roughwood Collection)

The Christmas Cook

children printed in 1843. Upon opening the metamorphosis, he is reduced to a skeleton, since death takes away all in the end. One can easily visualize the lecture that must have come with such a cookie when Mother was asked inquisitively who this man was. Many of the churches felt it necessary to provide a "Christian" explanation for these old images before they would accept them. Thus we see in the early part of the nineteenth century a large rewriting of Christmas along these lines.

THE HIGH CHURCH MOVEMENT AND THE CULT OF SAINT NICHOLAS

There always was a religious connection with the Christmas tree in the eyes of those who decorated it, buried as that connection may have been beneath layers upon layers of ideological veneer. In a 1597 reference to a Christmas tree at Türkheim in Alsace, there is mention of colored papers for flowers, apples, and communion wafers used as decoration.[9] The term actually used was *Hostien*, although elsewhere in later accounts of Christmas trees, we see the word *Oblaten*. *Oblaten* are made with a wafer iron. *Hostien*, however, are communion wafers; there is no doubt about the meaning of this word. Communion wafers may seem like a curious thing to hang on Christmas trees, but in this period they were often impressed with religious scenes and symbols, and therefore had a highly ornamental appearance.

On the other hand, it is not likely that a priest or Lutheran minister would allow his supply of communion wafers to be pilfered for such a purpose, not to mention the obvious sacrilege, considering what the wafers were intended for in a church service. Therefore, we must assume that the prevalent use of ornamental wafers on the earliest Christmas trees was based on a supply made at home.

The ownership of wafer irons was a mark of very high status; they were often given as wedding gifts. In the 1500s and 1600s, these were utensils found only in the kitchens of the well-to-do.[10] Taken in this context, a tree ostentatiously rigged out with multitudes of wafers was as much eye-catching and ornamental as it was a rather bald display of one's wealth and position. This further suggests that Christmas trees served a different purpose in the 1500s than later in their history, not that this mattered much to Sunday schools or to the High Church Movement of the nineteenth century.

The High Church Movement of the 1840s began earlier in England and quickly spread to this country among the Episcopalians and German-Reformed. From these two denominations, it fanned out into other churches. In essence, it was a theological approach to Protestantism that embraced the Romantic Movement in art and literature. It was a rediscovery of the Middle Ages as a repository of true Christianity. Therefore Gothic architecture was revived as an appropriate style for Protestant churches and ancient customs were seen in a new idealized light. Elaborate rituals formerly condemned as idolatrous and Romish were dusted off and reincorporated into denominational practice.

In Christmas, the movement found a bonanza in the buried customs of pre-Reformation England. Advent was thus rediscovered and given new emphasis. Advent wreaths, rare in colonial America, soon became a veritable symbol of the holiday season. Holly, mistletoe, crêches, caroling, Yorkshire pudding, Bakewell pudding, wassail, roast boars' heads, peacock pies, the list of Old English revivals is nearly endless. Everywhere in newspapers and popular literature these nostalgic themes raised their heads, aided by appealing illustrations from leading artists such as Cruickshank, Caldecott, and most of all, Thomas Nast. Nowhere did the success of this revival movement come together in a more universally accepted way than in the Christmas tree and Santa Claus.

The Christmas tree had been an element of the German-American Christmas for some time. But the High Church Movement, which for the German-Americans started at Mercersburg Seminary in Pennsylvania, found in it an extraordinary relic of supposedly medieval custom. Soon we see the tree appearing as a focus for Sunday school pageants, for the distribution of gifts to children at orphanages, and by degrees it assumes a more and more "public" character.

The Lutherans, also quick to recognize the missionary value of the Christmas tree, discovered in one of Luther's letters a passage

"The Christmas Tree," from an 1864 wood engraving. (Roughwood Collection)

about trees in Eden that they misidentified as Christmas trees.[11] This reference was the basis for depicting Luther beside a Christmas tree in many, many children's gift books throughout the nineteenth century. If the founder of Protestantism could have a Christmas tree in his study at Wittenberg, then of course it was easy enough for the other Protestant denominations to follow suit. This propaganda was extremely effective in giving the tree and all of its trimmings a lasting theological orthodoxy. But more than that, the tree became a symbol of American patriotism.

During the Civil War, the Christmas tree was widely treated as a symbol of hope for the reunification of the country. The tree as a symbol of hope was one of the new "Christian" meanings given to it by the Sunday School and High Church Movements. As an icon not then generally associated with Southern culture, and therefore free of any negative associations with slavery, the tree became a display case for national sentiment. This is evident in the 1865 advertisement of New York confectioner William Taylor, whose Christmas Saloon at 555 Broadway bulged with patriotic paraphernalia for the tree: "Toys of multifarious forms and devices, Miniature Military Equipments, Lincoln Log Cabins, Glass Balls, Reflectors, Candles, Flags, Fruit, Flowers . . . including everything required to decorate a Christmas Tree. Bon Bon Boxes, a beautiful assortment, in Silk, Velvet, Paper, and Fancy Wood. Flowers in Pots, Stuffed Birds, etc." [12]

For many years after the Civil War, patriotic emblems, such as flags, candy cannons, log cabins, Liberty Bells, and portraits of Lincoln in sugar were standard decorations on the American Christmas tree. Today we are not likely to use flags or guns, but in creating trees with ethnic themes, we have also continued this long and evolved process of Americanization. After all, what ethnic symbol has become more Americanized than Saint Nicholas?

Saint Nicholas was a popular winter saint among the New Netherlands Dutch, who celebrated his day on December 6, the day he is said to have died. On this day, small gifts, often gingerbread and other edibles, were distributed to children. In some houses Saint Nicholas left his gifts in wooden shoes; in others, on plates set on a table. The history of Saint Nicholas is especially long and tangled, and he is a figure with widely varying attributes in the different countries where he is venerated—not always in connection with the Christmas season.

In America, his celebration was centered in the Hudson Valley, and there mostly

Chocolate mold with an assortment of patriotic and secular Christmas motifs from the early 1870s. The potted flower (TOP RIGHT) represents a silk or paper auricula, once a popular ornament for the Christmas tree.

Martin Luther's Christmas Tree

among families of Dutch ancestry. Historically, he was a latent almost shadowy figure, not well known until writers such as Washington Irving fleshed him out into a jovial, colorful character from local history. On the other hand, Saint Nicholas was not only a Dutch saint. The first retelling of the legends of Saint Nicholas in a modern language (as opposed to Latin or Greek) was the Saint Nicholas poem by Robert Wace (ca. 1100–1174), written in England.[13] Saint Nicholas was not only known in medieval England; many churches and sanctuaries were built in his honor. He was also the patron of schoolboys and scholars, as well as the benign mascot of the Saint Nicholas Society centered in New York and Albany.

This society, which held anniversary festivals for Saint Nicholas around December 6 each year, consisted mostly of gentlemen descended from early New York families. The society's dinner in 1846, which was reported in *The Knickerbocker,* was held at city hall in New York and such well-known men as James DePeyster Ogden and Hamilton Fish were present. An address was given in Dutch, and the menu consisted of "the choicest 'relishes' of the old Dutch tables; 'sour-krout,' 'krullers,' 'speck and applejes,' 'olikoeks,' 'rolletjes,' and the like, never forgetting 'schnaps' and pipes."[14]

In New York, most of these foods were associated with Christmas and with one's Dutch colonial heritage, ethnic foods in the truest sense of the term. Outside New York and the Hudson Valley, crullers and *oli-koecks* in particular were absorbed into American Christmas cookery through popular association with these Saint Nicholas feasts, which were given wide coverage in the press. They received an added boost, however, by virtue of their assocation with the High Church Movement.

Among American Episcopalians, the High Church Movement centered around Bishop John Henry Hobart of New York City. Hobart was in fact the acknowledged leader of the entire movement in the United States. In restoring ancient ritual to the Episcopal Church, Hobart and his circle naturally looked with renewed interest at certain medieval saints and their traditions. The mantle of cultural archeologist, at least as far as Christmas was concerned, was assumed by one of Bishop Hobart's colleagues and a fellow parishioner, Clement C. Moore.

Inspired by the tenets of the High Church Movement, Moore discovered a suitably ancient relic in Saint Nicholas and revived him by casting him in a setting easily recognized by children. Like Robert Wace of old, he composed a Saint Nicholas poem, yet drew his material not from early medieval legends directly, but rather from Washington Irving and local folklore. In doing so, he created Santa Claus, a thoroughly American saint.

The New Netherlands contribution to the early American Christmas is represented here by New Years Cake (THE ORNAMENTED HEART AND THE ROUND CAKE ON THE SHELF), waffles, crullers (FOREGROUND) and *olie-koecken* fried in an *olie-koeck* pan.

The Christmas Cook

The immediate success of Moore's *Night Before Christmas* in 1840 is now history. Yet it is unlikely that without this popularization, his "jolly old elf" would ever have reached national acceptance. Most important, in terms of the culinary history of the American Christmas, with the coming of Santa Claus and the Christmas tree, we acquired two important ingredients to the holiday as we know it. In Santa Claus, we acquired a gift bringer known for culinary largesse; in the tree, we acquired a place to hang the food.

The influence of the High Church Movement is still with us today. One might suggest that in the re-Catholicizing of Christ-mas, its triumph has been complete. But other forces were also unleashed in the nineteenth century that tempered this victory and to some degree also derailed it. The most unforeseen of these has also proved to be the most formidable: commercialization.

Once the Christmas tree and Saint Nicholas were separated from their original denominational contexts, desectarianized so to speak; once they were accepted as happy, harmless ways to entertain children, yet at the same time serve as tools for "doing good," it was easy enough for the marketplace to do the rest. Saint Nicholas and the tree have now become worldwide cults.

"The Christmas Tree," from *Peterson's Magazine*, December 1851.
(Roughwood Collection)

The Christmas Cook

OBLATGEBACKENES, OR ROLLED WAFERS

Marcus Loofft's *Nieder-Sächsisches Koch Buch* (Lower Saxony Cook Book) was sold by German bookshops in this country during the eighteenth century. Today it is a rich source of recipes for the food historian. *Oblatgebackenes* (things wafer baked) is Loofft's quaint North German way of writing *Oblaten*. We are dealing of course with wafers, the edible ornaments that show up on the earliest Christmas trees in Germany.

The lasting popularity of wafer recipes in that country is evident in the recent success of Helga Tenschert's *Engelsbrot und Eisenkuchen* (Angel's Bread and Waffles), a Christmas cookbook devoted entirely to the art of making wafers and waffles with antique irons.[15]

You simply cannot do this recipe without a wafer iron. The batter cannot be used for pancakes or waffles because it must be pressed paper thin, otherwise it is like wood. If you have a pizzelle iron, you are set to proceed. If you have an electric pizzelle iron, follow my instructions for making the batter, but follow the manufacturer's directions for baking. If you have an antique wafer iron, you will need special advice. I have included it in my procedures below.

But before we begin, please take a look at your wafer iron. Make certain that it is perfectly clean and free of any old batter that might be lingering down in the pattern. Use a plastic darning needle or toothpick to clean it out, but do not scratch the metal. Old dry batter and deep scratches will give the wafer a spot to stick and you may have trouble getting it off. Also, be absolutely certain that your iron clamps shut *tightly,* particularly at the "front," that part of the iron directly opposite the handles. If the wafer iron does not clamp shut evenly, the pattern will be faint and part of the wafer will darken or brown before the rest is done. It may also leak batter, which only adds to the mess.

In the eighteenth century, when this recipe was written, the wafers were baked over intensely hot charcoal stoves, as I have shown in the photograph on page 67. I am grateful to Ernst Segschneider of the Cultural History Museum at Osnabrück, Germany, for actually showing me how this was done. You may use the burner on your kitchen range, preferably a gas burner. Take care to keep the burner free of any batter that may drip into it.

YIELD: APPROXIMATELY 2 DOZEN
6-INCH WAFERS.

continued

8 tablespoons (1 stick) unsalted butter
3½ cups all-purpose flour
1 cup sugar
2 tablespoons ground cardamom
2 teaspoons ground cinnamon

Grated zest of 1 lemon
1 cup milk or cream
3 whole eggs
3 egg yolks

Heat the butter until it foams. Skim off the foam and remove the butter from the heat. Sift the flour, sugar, cardamom, and cinnamon together twice; add the lemon zest. Make a hole in the center of the dry ingredients, add the clarified butter, stir, then add the milk or cream. Stir continuously until this begins to form crumbs.

Beat the eggs and yolks to a light froth and add them. Beat the batter vigorously until it becomes thick and ropy. The batter should run in a continuous string from the end of the mixing spoon or paddle.

Heat the wafer iron on both sides, open it, and grease it lightly. The grease should sizzle and smoke on *both* halves of the iron. Drop a large spoonful of batter on one of the halves. Keep it level and close it gently so that the batter cooks as it spreads. Clamp the iron shut and hold it over the heat, turning it from time to time so that the wafer bakes evenly. Allow roughly 3 minutes to each side. Once you become familiar with your iron and the way it transfers heat (each old iron seems to be slightly different in this re-spect), baking will begin to go more quickly. Do not despair if the first ones you make are imperfect.

To test for doneness, open the iron. If it pulls away from the wafer, the wafer is done on that side. Close the iron, turn it over and repeat the test on the other side. If the wafer is loose, it is ready to come out. Remove it from the iron and wrap it around the handle of a wooden spoon or a wooden cone. Once it cools, the wafer will become stiff and crisp. Or, cool it flat on a wire rack. Store in an airtight container.

NOTE: It is important to determine exactly how much batter your iron requires for 1 wafer. The size of wafer irons varies so that there is no firm rule to follow other than to run a few test wafers. It is better to underestimate than to waste batter. This will also save you the trouble of having to trim off the overflow, which usually burns before the wafer is done.

SOURCE: Marcus Loofft, *Nieder-Sächsisches Koch Buch* (Lübeck: Christian Iversen & Compagnie, 1778), 437.

Wafers were baked by holding the wafer iron over a charcoal stove.
The hot coals were held between grates inside the iron box. Both
stove and wafer iron date from about 1750.

OLIE-KOECKEN, OR KNICKERBOCKERS

1855

This delightful ball-shaped fritter or fat cake gained widespread popularity in American cookbooks in the nineteenth century. American cooks had trouble with the Dutch name, hence the almost endless—and sometimes confusing!—variations in spelling. In his study of New Jersey Dutch dialect, J. Dyneley Prince spelled it *oljekuk,* which was deemed correct New Netherlandish.[16] But New Netherlands also produced a subdialect called *Nexer Dauts* (Negro Dutch), which was spoken by slaves and servants and black cooks, thus we have even further vagaries of spelling to deal with. And no one has explained how these cakes also came to be called Knickerbockers. For simplicity's sake, I have chosen the Holland Dutch spelling used by Peter Rose in her excellent translation of *De Verstandige Kock (The Sensible Cook),* one of the most popular Dutch cookbooks of the seventeenth century. As Rose's research has pointed out, this cookbook is also the direct source for some of the oldest Hudson Valley *olie-koecken* recipes.[17]

One of the most famous of these was a recipe popularized by Elizabeth Van Rensselaer in the 1780s. It belonged to a family of recipes known more generally among the Hudson Valley Dutch as "the Albany Method," which might be best described as a 12-egg recipe, certainly the richest and most delectable of the many other recipes in circulation. My recipe, which is half the proportion of the original, is not Elizabeth Van Rensselaer's and not the Albany Method exactly, but a recipe that measures in at about two-thirds of the Albany proportions. Even by cutting it back by half the yield is enormous, far more than can be eaten in one evening. And, I might add, *olie-koecken* are at their best when they are fresh.

YIELD: APPROXIMATELY 5 DOZEN FRITTERS.

2 teaspoons active dry yeast
1 cup milk
12 tablespoons (1½ sticks) unsalted butter
½ cup sugar
4 eggs
1 teaspoon salt
5 cups all-purpose flour
Confectioners' sugar
Lard or vegetable oil

Heat ¼ cup milk to lukewarm; proof the yeast in the milk. Cream the butter and sugar. Beat the eggs to a froth, then beat in the remaining milk. Combine this with the butter and sugar. Add the salt and the proofed yeast, sift in the flour. Work this into a soft dough, cover, and set aside to double in bulk.

When the dough is ready, punch it down, and if it is too sticky to handle, dust your hands and the work surface with a little flour —2 tablespoons should do it. Knead well and form into walnut-size balls weighing ap-proximately 1 ounce. Let the balls of dough rest for 10 to 15 minutes, or until well risen.

While the balls of dough are rising, bring lard or vegetable oil in a deep fryer to 375°F. Add your dough balls and fry evenly until golden brown on all sides. Drain, cool, and roll in confectioners' sugar. These make a very attractive table decoration when stacked pyramid fashion and garnished with little sprigs of boxwood.

NOTE: Several nineteenth-century foundries in this country sold an implement they called an *olie-koeck* pan. Many signed examples bear the names of J. M. B. Davidson and Shear, Packard & Company of Albany, New York, or Griswold of Erie, Pennsyl-vania. This pan is the same as the egg and *Krapfen* pans made in Germany. There is an illustration of one on page 63 with *olie-koecken* in it. The method was quite simple and ensured that the balls of dough would be perfectly round. I call it the "low-fat" method.

Heat the pan on top of your stove and put ¼ teaspoon of lard or Crisco in each compartment. Let the fat come to a smoking boil, then add your balls of dough. Roll them occasionally so that they fry evenly on all sides. When golden brown, they are ready. Drain, cool, and roll in confectioners' sugar.

SOURCE: *Cookery as It Should Be* (Philadelphia: Willis Hazard, 1855), 173.

Martin Luther's Christmas Tree

Wishing You a Merry Christmas

Chromolithograph Christmas
card, American, circa 1880.
(Roughwood Collection)

WAFFLES, OR IRON CAKES

1660

Waffles were once an extremely popular Christmas dish, traced to the Netherlands, where they seem to have first developed. Many Dutch and Flemish paintings from the 1500s and 1600s show them, often in connection with Saint Nicholas Day.

Recipes for Dutch waffles begin to turn up in English cookbooks by the seventeenth century. This one comes from the manuscript receipt book of Frances Boothby, dated 1660. In it, she calls her waffles "iron cakes," which is a fairly approximate translation of one of their common North German names: *Eisenkuchen*. In the dialect of New Netherlands, they were called *aizekuken*.

Waffles were eaten in most parts of early America during colonial times, but they were eaten only on holidays. With the coming of the cookstove in the nineteenth century and the waffle iron sets that were often

Waffle and wafer irons from the nineteenth century.

sold with them, waffles lost their special festiveness. They quickly shifted from a Christmas and New Years food to something made more generally for Sunday dinner. In spite of its seventeenth-century origins, the batter in this recipe can be used in any standard electric waffle iron.

Otherwise, the baking technique is basically the same as that for wafers, the only difference being that I suggest using a small trivet on which to rest the iron above the burner on your stove. Something 2 to 3 inches above the heat source would be ideal. I would also recommend that you refer to my remarks about preparing a wafer iron for baking below.

YIELD: APPROXIMATELY 6 LARGE WAFFLES.

2 cups milk
2 teaspoons active dry yeast
8 tablespoons (1 stick) butter
4 eggs

1 cup white bread crumbs
1¾ cups all-purpose flour
Sugar and cinnamon

Warm the milk. Reserve 1 cup and proof the yeast in it. Melt the butter in the remaining milk. When the yeast is proofed, combine it with the milk and butter. Beat the eggs to a light froth and add them to the milk. Add the bread crumbs and the flour and beat thoroughly to make a thick, rich batter. Cover and let rise until bubbles form on the surface.

Heat the waffle iron on both sides. Open it and grease it with a brush dipped in melted butter or cooking fat. Then close it and heat it evenly on both sides. When the iron begins to smoke, it is ready to use.

Fill the bottom half of the iron with batter, allowing about 1 cup of batter per waffle. Clamp it shut and bake the waffle on both sides (roughly 4 minutes per side). Trim off any excess batter with a sharp knife before removing the waffle from the iron. Cool on racks.

To serve, sprinkle each waffle with sugar and cinnamon. They are delicious with Snow Ice Cream (page 47).

SOURCE: Frances Boothby, "Her Booke of Cockery" (Unpublished manuscript, Essex, England: 1660), Recipe 79. Roughwood Collection.

FOUR

The Pastry Cook's Companion

The previous chapters have provided us with a general overview of Christmas feasting in terms of the ideas that shaped it and the days and customs that encouraged such monumental efforts in the kitchen. We have also touched on a number of the traditional dishes associated with aspects of the holiday now largely forgotten: Twelfth Night Cake, Preacher Pie, and Oli-Koecks, to name three.

In the following chapters, we will turn our attention to specific groups of Christmas desserts with the clear understanding that in many cases distinctions are vague and one group often blends into the next. The subject here is cake, and this leads us directly into murky water over the very meaning of the word.

It is possible, for example, to define the Fruit Pound Cake and Dutch Cake in this chapter as a baked pudding and a bread, respectively, and the Little Plumcakes in chapter 5 as a cookie. Let it be said that early American cooks were not in this case imprecise about terminology; they simply allowed that cake covered broader territory than it does today.

"Cookie" has taken over the workload for "little cake." On the other hand, "gingerbread" now generally means to most Ameri-

Ripe quinces and gooseberries put up in earthen jars are ready for Christmas pies. Susannah Carter's Paste Royal (PAGE 94) lines the tartlet dish (CENTER), while Marmalade of Quinces (PAGES 204–205) is shown cut into lozenge shapes (BOTTOM RIGHT), a popular Christmas candy in the eighteenth century.

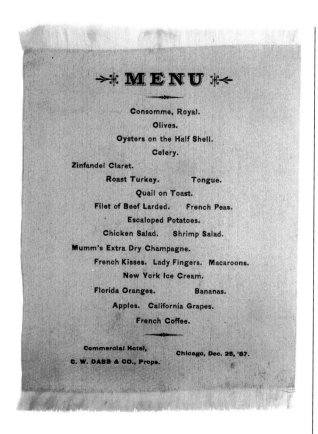

⋇✳ M E N U ✳⋇

Consomme, Royal.

Olives.

Oysters on the Half Shell.

Celery.

Zinfandel Claret.

Roast Turkey. Tongue.

Quail on Toast.

Filet of Beef Larded. French Peas.

Escaloped Potatoes.

Chicken Salad. Shrimp Salad.

Mumm's Extra Dry Champagne.

French Kisses. Lady Fingers. Macaroons.

New York Ice Cream.

Florida Oranges. Bananas.

Apples. California Grapes.

French Coffee.

Commercial Hotel,
C. W. DABB & CO., Props. Chicago, Dec. 25, '87.

Menu printed on silk for the Commercial Hotel in Chicago, Christmas 1887. Note that California red zinfandel was the featured wine for this dinner and that Florida oranges and bananas were considered dessert luxuries. (Roughwood Collection)

cans a soft raised cake flavored with ginger and molasses. In the eighteenth century, prior to the evolution of recipes such as New Orleans Gingerbread, all Christmas gingerbreads were cookies, rather soft when made with honey, definitely crisp when made with molasses. Since the next chapter deals with Christmas cookies and the evolution of their

decoration, let us look more closely at the raised cake and the complex problems facing us when we undertake to reproduce even the most uncomplicated recipes. But first, it would be useful to know what kinds of cakes were most popular. Essentially, they fell into two categories: cakes raised with eggs and cakes raised with yeast. Cakes requiring eggs were the most expensive. Chemical leaveners were introduced to eliminate both eggs and yeast.

A long and chatty discourse on preparations for Christmas dinner in Philadelphia's *The Post* for December 20, 1828, observed: "The careful dame is anxiously employed in superintending the manufacture of pastry and pudding, and the younger ladies glow with the heat of baking pound cake, and fruit cake—ladies' fingers and jumbles." There we have it, the four most popular luxury cakes in the 1820s.

If cupcakes were also known as Poor Man's Pound Cake (page 37), they must have been the recipe of cheaper choice in households where cost counted. More affluent cooks made the real thing. I have supplied at the end of this chapter an American pound cake recipe that I consider classic. And to illustrate how Christmas pound cake could accumulate "plumbs" and come out of the oven as Fruit Pound Cake, I have provided an excellent example from Kentucky.

But ladyfingers you ask? I never would have suspected that one either. And yet, there on the menu—many years later—for President Harrison's 1890 Christmas dinner

Sugar nippers broke loaf sugar into "lump" sugar (BOTTOM LEFT),
which was then pounded in a mortar or rolled with a glass
rolling pin to make powdered sugar.

Sweetmeats were put up in glass or earthenware jars or in glass
"tumblers" like the one on the right containing greengage plums
in syrup. In the glass jar (CENTER), is Candied Orange Peel
(PAGES 194–195). Caribbean sweetmeats for the North American trade
were packed in jars set inside small wooden boxes, like the
guava jelly box (FOREGROUND) from Matanzas, Cuba, circa 1800.

at the White House, we find among the mincemeat pies, the ice cream, and the tutti-frutti, macaroons, wafers, American Plum Pudding and *ladyfingers*.[1] Were they still in fashion? Or was this another case of Colonial Revival? Suspicious, I delved into cookbooks—printed and handwritten—from the colonial period. There they are, like doves in a row, recipes by the hundreds, except that ladyfingers in those days were called *Naples Biscuits,* cakes, incidentally, with a texture far superior to most of their commercial progeny today. I would suggest that the underlying reason for this was careful choice of ingredients, which brings us back to the warning signals raised earlier about cake baking in general.

I suppose the best place to begin is with the sweetmeats, since they were the most debatable of the basic ingredients—after all fruitcake was not fruitcake without them.

ARE SWEETMEATS INDISPENSABLE?

We use them in fruitcake and Twelfth Night Cake. We put them in Preacher's Pie and mincemeat. We shred them up and add them to gingerbread. We eat them as candy, as in Glacé Fruits or Marmalade of Quinces. These are foods preserved in sugar—dry, like crystallized ginger; sticky, like candied citron; or wet, like cherries in syrup. All of these are sweetmeats and indispensable to Christmas cookery. We do not appreciate today the difficulties once involved in making them, not that there wasn't occasional rebellion.

A writer, who identified herself only as Frances, submitted a lengthy tirade against sweetmeats to the New York Methodist newspaper *Christian Advocate and Journal:*

> Let us not stint the growth of our children or give our friends dyspepsia, or deprive ourselves of the pleasure of reading useful books or periodicals, by lavishing our time and money "for that which is not bread, and our labor for that which satisfieth not." Let us follow the example of some of the New England farmers in the temperance reformation, who say they will no longer fill their cellars with cider to make drunkards of their children and neighbors. Let us say that we will not make epicures of our children by needless expenditure in articles of food . . . every englightened Christian mother will see at a glance that she is doing far better for her children to give them a useful periodical, than prepare them a jar of sweetmeats, or make them a luscious fruit, or pound cake.[2]

Frances was right about the labor. In 1838, it was not enough to go to the store and buy sugar. There were many different grades of sugar, and they came in cones called loaves. Loaf sugar had to be broken, then pounded. Pounded or rolled sugar made a powder, which was not the same as the confectioners' sugar of today. Confectioners' sugar is to confectionery what flour is to baking, as you will see in chapter 7.

Old-style powdered or rolled sugar was the equivalent of the expensive grade of sugar sold in this country today as *superfine, bar sugar,* or *dessert sugar.* It is this grade of sugar that was generally used in making cakes. It is also called for in the recipe for Paste Royal on page 94. It weighs the same as granulated sugar, cup for cup, but produces an entirely different texture in cakes. It is also not as sweet, or at least, it seems that way to our sense of taste.

For sweetmeats, the broken loaf sugar had to be melted, skimmed of impurities, and re-crystallized, a tedious task that is often explained in detail in household books and cookbooks of the period.[3] Fortunately, today we can avoid this work because sugar is already processed for us when we buy it in the store. The trade-off is that the big sugar concerns have vastly diminished our selection of sugars. They do not want to be bothered with so-called boutique sugars; therefore, we cannot recreate many of the rich flavors of the past. We cannot, for example, obtain coarse-grained yellow sugar, muscovado sugar, or brown sugar crystals in most American supermarkets even though these commodities are commonly available in Britain.

The same problems apply to flour, perhaps even more so. Rural households had their own flour ground at local mills. They would take so many bushels of wheat to the mill (usually 2 or 3) and in return take home a precalculated amount of flour. I say precalculated because the miller knew how many pounds of flour came from a bushel of wheat.

The flour that the farmer took home was not necessarily ground from the same wheat he gave the mill because he took in only a few bushels and the mill was usually running most of the week, grinding large amounts of flour for many different customers. The reason for taking such small amounts of grain to the mill was simple: the grain could be stored in a barn or granary, but the flour, once ground, would spoil. Therefore, one did not keep on hand in the house any more flour than absolutely necessary.

People who lived at a distance from mills or who lived in towns bought barrel flour. The yield from a barrel of flour varied with the type of wheat used to make the flour. Some large mills, like the Brandywine Mills owned by the Leas near Wilmington, Delaware, produced "family flour" for general home use. It was a blend of hard and soft wheat, the equivalent of all-purpose flour today. "Lea's Best," one of the most famous of these early all-purpose flours, was introduced in 1742. It is no longer manufactured.

In an article on flour in *The Household* in 1874, the following statistics were published to show what one cook squeezed out of her single barrel of family flour: 34 loaves of bread, 17 6-quart pans of doughnuts, 17 messes of biscuits, 94 pies, 7 loaf cakes, 1½ dozen tart crusts, 3 dozen gingersnaps, and 1 mess of pancakes.[4] This represents the flour consumption in one household for roughly one month during the peak baking season. We do not know how many persons this household included (I suspect 6 to 8). Re-

Brandywine Mills near Wilmington, Delaware, circa 1840. From a painting
attributed to Bass Otis. (Courtesy of the Historical Society of Delaware)

gardless, we can easily see that bread, pies, and doughnuts took precedence over most other baked goods and that cookies were a much lower priority than the large supply of biscuits, such as buttermilk biscuits, beaten biscuits, or milk biscuits.

The eighteen tart crusts represent fruit pies, the kind with latticework or crumb tops. I would suggest that among those eighteen at least some were cranberry of the sort discussed in the cranberry tart recipe in this chapter. The crust recipes I have provided

will give you a clearer idea of the differences in flour requirements between pies and tarts.

Of course, our statistics deal with a New England household, thus they reflect highly regionalized eating habits, and we have no way of knowing whether this family was Congregationalist or what emphasis it placed on Christmas feasting.

Manuscript cookbooks in particular are often top-heavy with cake recipes, many of which were indeed prepared only at Christmas. I like the following letter to the editors of *The Household* because it describes in her own words what a homemade cookbook meant to one busy housekeeper in 1874:

> I have made me a nice cook-book of recipes taken from THE HOUSEHOLD. I take from my papers, as fast as they come, all the recipes that I want to save, and paste them in a blank book that I keep for that purpose, and then I do not have to lose any time or patience looking for them when wanted. I have quite a book full, and all of them good, which is more than can be said of the recipes in some cook-books that are sold.[5]
>
> —*Mrs. H. J. H.*

The last sentence is telling. Historically, many women preferred their own recipe collections to printed cookbooks because their own collections were closest to their lifestyle in terms of selection and usefulness. Most cookbooks had some recipes they liked, and many that they did not. Cookbooks were expensive, often costing more than three dollars. Yet that was no guarantee against their becoming dead wood in the kitchen, like shoes that do not exactly fit.

Of course, there were Christmas cookbooks brought out specially for the season. Mrs. Bliss's *The Practical Cook Book* was first reviewed in *M'Makin's Model American Courier* for November 16, 1850, under the headline "Christmas Cooking."[6] But Mrs. Bliss represents a different level of Christmas cookery because she is in a consumer relationship with her readers. After all, she was a professional confectioner and pastry chef in Boston. Her book was a real Christmas gift, something as much for the kitchen as for the parlor, a book fun to read by someone who loved to cook. The ancient grease and egg spots in my copy speak volumes.

Most women, however, clipped recipes from such magazines as *The Household* or from newspapers and almanacs, or from the little pamphlet cookbooks distributed by grocers at Christmas. The *Housekeeper's Friend*, printed in Boston in 1879 as an almanac cookbook for 1880, is full of cake recipes and is typical of this genre.[7] It is not until you read it closely that you realize it was published for Joseph Burnett & Company, and that Burnett's leading product was vanilla flavoring.

Various cake and tart pans from the eighteenth and nineteenth centuries. The tin Strietzel mold (BOTTOM RIGHT) was used to bake the Dutch Cake recipe on PAGE 96.

The Pastry Cook's Companion

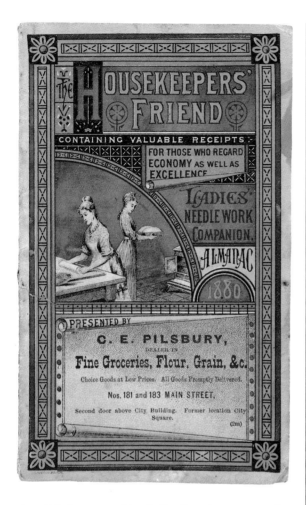

An 1880 almanac cookbook distributed to agents and customers of the Joseph Burnett Company of Boston, Christmas 1879. (Roughwood Collection)

Housewives received the cookbook from the grocer when they bought a large bottle of vanilla, thus it is a product promotional cookbook. This is how many recipes using vanilla found their way into the countryside and how many Christmas recipes reached audiences eager for novelty and the latest thing in festive baking.

Novelty eventually pushed aside the older forms of cake, in particular Dutch Cake and its relatives made with sweetened bread dough. Dutch Cake evolved in the Middle Atlantic states as perhaps the most popular of all Christmas cakes. During the Christmas season, it was even hawked on the street in small loaves priced especially for children.

The term *Dutch* refers in this case to the Germans who evidently introduced the cake in the early eighteenth century from Saxony to what is now East Germany. Structurally, Dutch Cake is nearly identical to the German Christmas Stollen, except that it was baked either in round loaves (like bread) or in Turk's cap molds. The latter form seems to have been the most popular in early American home cookery.

Christmas Dutch Cake illustrated on page 96 was sold from Boston to Savannah and as far west as Minneapolis. It went by multitudes of local or descriptive names—rusks, turkey buns, Stollen, Strietzel, to name a few —and often appeared on the table at other times of the year. In the 1830s, it was a popular dessert for formal picnics and was generally served with rose champagne, a custom kept alive by some Philadelphia and New York families into this century. Like pound cake, ladyfingers, fruitcake, and jumbles, Dutch cake was a symbol of Christmas feasting that spread Christmas through all the seasons of the year.

NAPLES BISCUITS, OR LADYFINGERS

1770

The proportions given here are half the original recipe.

YIELD: 80 LADYFINGERS.

6 eggs, separated
1 cup sugar
12 tablespoons all-purpose flour

2 tablespoons rosewater
4 drops oil of bitter almond, or mixed spices (optional)

Preheat the oven to 375°F.

Cream the yolks until lemon color and very thick, then beat in the sugar. Beat this until it begins to lighten. Gradually sift in the flour, alternating with a little rosewater, to keep the batter moist and light. Beat the whites until stiff peaks form and gently fold them into the batter. Add flavoring, such as oil of bitter almond or powdered spices, if desired.

Fill 80 greased ladyfinger forms with the batter and bake 12 to 15 minutes in the preheated oven. Let the cakes cool slightly before lifting them from the pans.

NOTE: These unflavored biscuits were used extensively in the eighteenth century to make puddings and other dessert dishes.

SOURCE: Richard J. Hooker, ed., *A Colonial Plantation Cookbook: The Receipt Book of Harriot Pinckney Horry, 1770.* (Columbia, S.C.: University of South Carolina Press, 1984), 104. Quoted with the kind permission of the publisher.

A ladyfinger pan beneath a Naples biscuit pan, both circa 1870.

In her original recipe, Amelia Simmons suggested baking the cake in a "slow oven 15 minutes." We can deduce from this that she was baking the batter in small tins. Likewise, a correspondent to *The Household* many years later remarked about her pound cake recipe: "Bake in tin hearts and rounds or add currants and bake in a loaf."[8] Mrs. Bliss called pound cake baked in heart-shaped tins *New York Heart Cakes*.[9] This was a Christmas variation of the once popular *Queen Cake*, a tea cake that came into English cookery in the seventeenth century. The cakes pictured on page 27 have been decorated with sugar in the style of the 1820s.

YIELD: ONE 10-INCH LOAF, 15 TO 20 SERVINGS.

> 1 pound (4 sticks) unsalted butter
> 2 cups superfine sugar
> 10 eggs
> 1 tablespoon grated nutmeg
> 3½ cups all-purpose flour
> ½ cup rosewater (see note)

Preheat the oven to 350°F.

Cream the butter until it is fluffy, then gradually beat in the sugar. Beat the eggs until thick and creamy; combine with the butter mixture. Add the nutmeg and gradually sift in the flour. Add the rosewater and beat the batter only enough to combine the rosewater; over-beating will drive it out.

Grease a 10-inch loaf pan and fill with the batter. Bake 50 to 60 minutes in the preheated oven. Cool on a rack before serving. This cake can also be frozen for later use.

NOTE: Historically, loaf-shaped pound cake was round like the old-fashioned loaves of bread. It was not iced because it was served like bread with butter and fruit jams. The small, ornamental cakes such as the hearts were generally iced—often elaborately—and served with sweet wines.

The rosewater is important in this recipe, both for flavor and for texture. It bakes out, leaving only a trace of sweetness. It also helps break down gluten in the flour because it contains alcohol, which of course lightens the cake. Lebanese rosewater is sold in large bottles in many shops that sell Greek foods. If you do not have rosewater, use ½ cup of cognac or peach brandy.

SOURCE: Amelia Simmons, *American Cookery* (Hartford: Hudson & Goodwin, 1796), 37.

Tin Queen Cake pans (TOP THREE) and a pan for New York Heart Cake.

Wishing you a
merry Christmas

Merry
Christmas to you

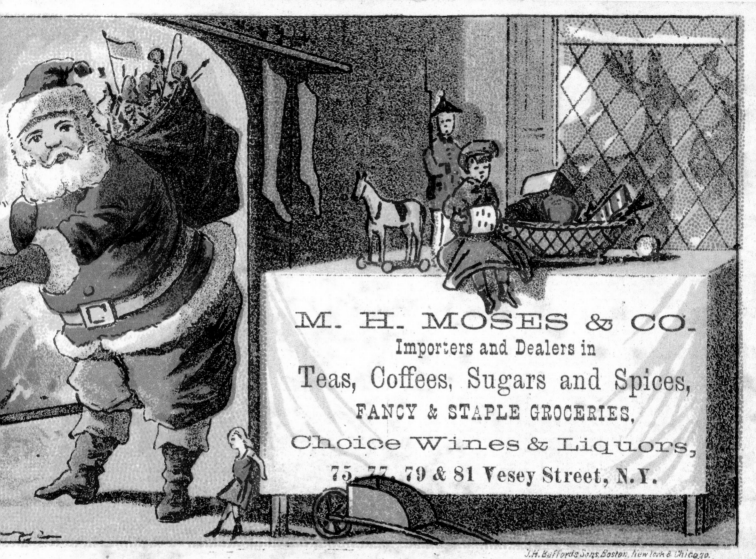

Chromolithograph trade card (ABOVE) and Christmas postcards, late 19th-century. Roughwood Collection

CRANBERRY TART

1848

Cranberries were popular for winter pies, and there is a great deal of advice in nineteenth-century household literature on how to keep them from spoiling. One writer suggested: "Cranberries will keep all winter in a firkin of water in a cellar."[10] A firkin in this case is a straight-sided crock.

Another writer commented: "Cranberry pie is better with cake spread in place of a top crust. Any cake we happen to be making will do."[11] This creation is now called Cranberry Sponge Pie. You may use the pound cake batter in the preceding recipe, allowing about 1 cup of batter for each 9-inch pie.

In Pennsylvania, we preferred crumb toppings. Since this is a Pennsylvania recipe, I have included my grandmother's recipe for crumb topping.

YIELD: ONE 9-INCH PIE, 6 TO 8 SERVINGS.

1 batch My Paste Royal (page 95)
4 cups (1 pound) cranberries
1 cup water
2 cups brown sugar
¼ cup lemon juice
Grated zest of 1 orange
2 teaspoons grated nutmeg
Rum-flavored whipped cream
for garnish

Preheat the oven to 425°F.

Line a pie dish with the paste royal. Simmer the cranberries with the water, sugar, lemon juice, orange zest, and nutmeg for 15 to 20 minutes, or until the berries begin to soften. Fill the pie shell with the stewed fruit mixture. Cover with a latticework crust or crumb topping. Bake in the preheated oven 40 to 45 minutes.

Allow the pie to cool after baking so that it will set. Serve cold with rum-flavored whipped cream. If you choose to bake in tartlet shells—which I prefer for this recipe—allow approximately 15 minutes of baking time at 425°F.

Earthenware tartlet pans made at Salem, North Carolina, 1815–1830. (Courtesy of Old Salem, Inc.)

GRACE HICKMAN WEAVER'S CRUMB TOPPING

YIELD: SUFFICIENT FOR ONE 9-INCH PIE.

8 heaping tablespoons flour
7 tablespoons ground almonds
6 tablespoons cold unsalted butter

6 tablespoons sugar
Nutmeg

Using two knives, cut or chop the flour, ground almonds, butter, and sugar to a fine crumb. Scatter evenly over the top of the pie. Bake as directed above. Grate nutmeg over the top of the pie after it is baked.

SOURCE: Gustav Sigismund Peters, ed., *Die Geschickte Hausfrau* (Harrisburg, Pa.: Lutz & Scheffer, 1848), 17.

Cranberry picking, Ocean County, New Jersey, November 1877. (Roughwood Collection)

FRUIT POUND CAKE

— 1841 —

I think Mrs. Bryan called this Fruit Pound Cake because, like pound cake, it was one of the recipes she used for making pyramids of cakes, a subject that I take up in chapter 8 under table centerpieces. Mrs. Bryan's Fruit Pound Cakes were round, like the ones shown in the 1871 chromolithograph on the opposite page. This pyramid consists of 3 separate cakes of graduating sizes ornamented with icing and paste sugar decorations.

YIELD: ONE 8½-INCH DIAMETER CAKE, 10 TO 12 SERVINGS.

1 cup candied citron
1½ cups currants
1½ cups white raisins
2 cups peach brandy, or 1 cup brandy
  and 1 cup amaretto
½ pound (2 sticks) unsalted butter
2 cups superfine sugar
6 eggs

¼ cup white wine
2 tablespoons rosewater
1 tablespoon grated nutmeg
1½ teaspoons ground mace
1½ teaspoons ground cinnamon
1¾ cups all-purpose flour
2 cups sliced blanched almonds
Brandy

Chop the candied citron into small shreds. Mix it with the currants and raisins and add the peach brandy. Stir and cover. Let this infuse overnight, or until most of the liquid is absorbed.

Preheat the oven to 275°F.

Cream the butter and sugar until light. Beat the eggs to a froth and combine with the butter and sugar mixture. Add the wine, rosewater, and spices. Sift in the flour and beat to make a rich batter. Mix the almonds with the infused fruit, and fold them into the batter.

Grease a deep 10-inch diameter tube pan and line the bottom with baking parchment. Pour in the batter and bake 3 hours in the preheated oven. Remove cake from pan, and cool on a rack. When cool remove the paper.

Once the cake is cool, dip some cheesecloth in brandy and wrap the cake with it. Then wrap in aluminum foil and store in a cool place for 3 months before serving.

NOTE: James W. Parkinson gave this advice in 1881 about aging fruitcakes.

Those intended for the Christmas festivities should be made at or about the first of October; then put the cake into a round tin box, half an inch larger in diameter than the cake; then pour over it a bottle of the best brandy mixed with a pint of pure lemon, raspberry, strawberry or simple syrup, and one or more bottles of cham-

The Christmas Cook

pagne. Now put on the lid of the box, and have it carefully soldered on, so as to make all perfectly air-tight. Put it away in your store-room, and let stand till Christmas, only reversing the box occasionally, in order that the liquors may permeate the cake thoroughly.

This heroic treatment causes the ingredients to amalgamate, and the flavors to harmonize and blend more freely; and when on Christmas day, you bring out this hermit, after doing a three months' penance in a dark cell, it will come out rich, succulent and unctuous.[12]

Use a can opener to open the tin box.

SOURCE: Mrs. Lettice Bryan, *The Kentucky Housewife* (Cincinnati: Stereotyped by Shepard & Stearns, 1841), 281.

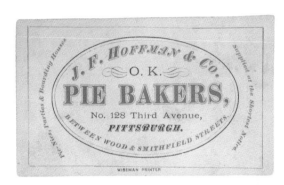

The Pastry Cook's Companion

PASTE ROYAL FOR PATTYPANS

1772

This is a rich crust that was particularly well liked for small ornamental pies and tartlets in the eighteenth century. However, it will become tough if handled too much. The texture should be somewhat similar to a butter cookie.

YIELD: APPROXIMATELY TWO DOZEN 3-INCH PATTYPANS.

½ pound (2 sticks) unsalted butter
3½ cups all-purpose flour
¼ cup superfine sugar

4 egg yolks
4 tablespoons dry white wine

Grate or chop the butter into the flour and sugar. Rub this mixture through a sieve until a fine crumb is formed. Make a hole in the center. Beat the yolks and the wine and pour into the hole. Take a large wooden fork and work this into a dough, handling it as little as possible.

Roll out the dough on a surface lightly dusted with flour, or between sheets of wax paper, and line the tartlet pans. For small pattypans and tartlets, this dough will bake in 20 to 25 minutes when the oven is preheated to 350°F. This rule of thumb applies to most fillings.

SOURCE: Susannah Carter, *The Frugal Housewife, or Complete Woman Cook* (Boston: Edes and Gill, 1772), 111.

Fruit Pound Cakes stacked into a pyramid and decorated with paste sugar ornaments. From an 1871 chromolithograph. (Roughwood Collection)

MY PASTE ROYAL

1990

*T*his is a family recipe that I use whenever I need to make up a batch of pies quickly. It gives a very delicate crust and works especially well for tartlet shells.

YIELD: SUFFICIENT FOR ONE 9-INCH PIE WITH TOP CRUST.

2⅔ cups pastry flour
8 tablespoons (1 stick) cold unsalted butter
3 tablespoons shortening
1 egg yolk
3 tablespoons dry white wine

*P*ut the flour in a large sieve. Cut the butter into bits and scatter over the flour. Add the shortening. Rub this to a soft, fluffy crumb through the sieve. Beat the yolk and the wine together. Make a hole in the center of the crumbs and add the egg mixture. Taking a large wooden fork, stir the crumbs and the liquid until balls of dough roughly the size of lima beans form. Do not touch the dough.

Spread half of the crumbs in the center of the righthand half of a 24-inch sheet of wax paper. Fold the lefthand part over the crumbs, and roll out the dough, taking care to roll only in one direction, away from the crease. Pull back the folded side of the wax paper and turn the dough out into your pie plate. Repeat this procedure for the top crust. Crimp and bake as required. This crust can be used for the cranberry tart recipe on page 90, the Preacher Pie on page 46, and most of the other pie recipes in this book. It was also used to make the crust of the Methodist Mincemeat pie shown on page 43.

DUTCH CAKE

1824

This Dutch Cake recipe comes to us from the recipe book of Hannah Marshall Haines, who called her cake Turkey Bun in reference to the fact that she baked it in a Turk's cap mold. The steel engraving on page 98, from the December 1875 issue of *Peterson's Magazine,* shows Dutch Cake in its Turkey Bun shape. For variation, I have baked this recipe in a tin Strietzel mold, which gives the cake a braided appearance. This cake is featured in the photograph on the opposite page. The actual mold is illustrated on page 82.

YIELD: 8 TO 10 SERVINGS.

¼ cup superfine sugar
1¼ cups warm milk
2 teaspoons active dry yeast
8 tablespoons (1 stick) unsalted butter
2 eggs
4½ to 5 cups all-purpose flour

3 tablespoons currants
1 teaspoon ground cinnamon
2 teaspoons ground nutmeg
2 tablespoons rosewater
Fine bread crumbs

Dissolve the sugar in the warm milk. Proof the yeast in the sugar and milk mixture. Cream the butter until fluffy. Beat the eggs to a froth, combine with the proofed yeast and add the creamed butter. Sift in 2½ cups of flour and beat to form a thick batter. Cover and set away to rise until double in bulk.

Preheat the oven to 350°F. Stir down the raised batter and add the currants, spices, rosewater, and remaining flour. Work this into a soft dough.

Liberally grease a 10- to 12-inch Turk's cap mold. Dust the inside with bread crumbs so that it is entirely coated. Form the dough into a ring and gently lay it in the mold. Cover and allow the dough to rise in a warm place until raised above the edge of the mold.

Bake 45 to 50 minutes, or until the cake sounds hollow when it is tapped.

Remove the cake from the mold and set it on a baking sheet. Put it back in the oven for 10 minutes to finish browning the crust. Cool on a rack. Serve plain without icing, as you would raisin bread.

SOURCE: Hannah Marshall Haines, "Receipt Book," unpublished manuscript (Philadelphia, 1811–1824), unpaginated. Quoted with the kind permission of the Wyck Association.

Dutch Cake baked in a mold in the shape of a Strietzel (braided loaf). Beside it (ON THE PLATTER), Queen Cakes decorated with sugar, and gooseberry, currant, and Cranberry Tartlets made with Susannah Carter's Paste Royal for Patty Pans (PAGE 94). See PAGE 90 for the cranberry recipe.

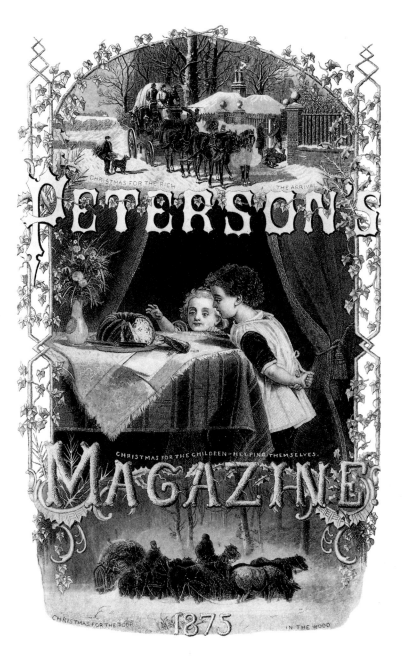

An 1875 engraving showing a Dutch Cake baked as a Turkey Bun.
(Roughwood Collection)

CRUST FOR RAISED PIES

1787

This recipe is one-eighth the original proportion, which means that in 1787 we would have started with 4 pounds of butter, 12 pounds of flour, and so forth. This ought to give you some idea of the enormous quantity of crust required for making raised pies in that period.

Raised pies were naturally quite festive and cooks often lavished them with great attention to exterior ornamentation. This crust, however, puffs somewhat as it bakes and is therefore better suited for sturdy, simple crusts of the sort pictured in the painting by Pieter Claesz on page 159. In fact, this recipe, cut to one-eighth, will produce enough dough to make a pie the size of the one shown in his painting.

YIELD: ENOUGH FOR A PIE APPROXIMATELY 10 INCHES IN DIAMETER, 4 TO 6 INCHES HIGH.

½ pound (2 sticks) unsalted butter
3 tablespoons lard, Crisco, or suet (see note)
4½ cups all-purpose flour
1 cup boiling water

Rub the butter and lard into the flour. Make a hole in the center of the crumbs and add the boiling water. Work this into a dough and knead like bread until soft and pliant. Chill 30 minutes, then roll out and use as required.

You may bake the crust separately and fill it later. In this case, preheat the oven to 400°F and roll out the dough in a thick sheet no thinner than ½". Cut out a circular base and a side strip and set the base on a baking sheet. Erect the side of the pie by attaching the side strip to the base and pressing it closed along the seams. Then fill the pie shell with rice. Form the lid or top crust by cutting out a piece of dough the same size as the base. Lay this over the rice and ornament it, but do not close the seams. An inverted plate the same size as the pie base may be used to support the lid so that it does not lose its shape during baking. Bake the filled pie shell 15 to 20 minutes, or until brown, then reduce the heat to 350°F and bake approximately 35 minutes.

NOTE: If the interior of the crust is brushed with egg white before it is filled with rice, the egg will seal the pie. The pie can then be emptied and filled with cooked fruit or roast chicken and gravy in the manner of the seventeenth century.

The original recipe called for suet where I have used lard. Mutton suet was often preferred for this purpose. For directions on preparing suet, refer to the mincemeat recipe on pages 178–179.

SOURCE: Charlotte Mason, *The Ladies' Assistant* (London: J. Walter, 1787), 355.

Beware of Camels

Christmas was always a season for busy hands, large and small. One can easily visualize Fred cutting meticulous paper animals for the tree, while his sister traces them out in dough. And perhaps, if their father were experienced with metal, he might transfer some of Fred's awkward creatures into tin as a memento of the family effort. Mother, of course, had the joy of baking the handiwork.

It would be pleasant to imagine that this picture—which is drawn directly from a Victorian children's book—measured up to reality. The fact is, tin cutters and similar ornamental equipment were once expensive, and until the 1880s and the appearance of mass-produced utensils of this kind, lucky was the household that possessed them. As we shall soon see, specialized tools, whether tin cutters, wooden cake prints, or ornamental molds, were more commonly the property of professional cooks and confectioners.

One need only peruse eighteenth- and early nineteenth-century cookbooks used by the well-to-do to spot the many ingenious ways cooks dealt with such shortages. For her Crisp Ginger Cake (page 147), Eliza Smith advised "cut it with a glass" (by which she meant a tumbler). Cookbook au-

A three-hundred-year evolution in cookie making is represented, from the seventeenth century Springerle angel (REAR LEFT), the 1860s style gingerbread herald with trumpet (CENTER), and the 1890s Yule Dollie (REAR RIGHT), to the coconut camel from the World War I era. The small cookies are decorated in the style of Joseph Angerer's early 1900s baking manual.

thor Hannah Glasse mentioned "a tea-cup or small glass"—even a wineglass would do.[1] Another technique was to use the lid of a tin tea canister, or anything else circular with a sharp edge.

From the frequency of such references in standard culinary works, it is clear that most cookbook authors presumed their readers were not likely to own tin cookie cutters or elegant molds. The basic tools for the Christ-

Before the appearance of inexpensive commercial tin cutters in the 1880s, the most common way to make animal cookies was to trace paper cutouts in dough. From a nineteenth-century wood engraving. (Roughwood Collection)

mas cook were a sharp knife and a pair of hands. Let us be generous and add a pie crimper and rolling pin, since Americans, as lovers of pies, would have considered both a necessity, and both, after all, are easily homemade. Where does this leave us in terms of traditional American Christmas pastries, let us say, prior to 1880?

As I have already explained in the previous chapter, most early American cookies were referred to as "cakes," and gingerbread was assumed to be a form of cookie, as in *Lebkuchen,* a gingerbread cookie made with honey. I have adhered to these older terms both here in my discussion of cookie baking and in the old recipe names. It is a usage that crops up frequently in historical sources, as in the following description of Mrs. Ring and her baking talents in an 1860s children's book called *Christmas with the Girls:*

> From pantry to table, and from table to pantry, she stepped again and again, until from the oven she drew out pans of dainty little cakes light and crisp and done to a turn. The most of them were simple round cakes, such as one might eat on any day of the year, but there were others—shapes of pigs with currants stuck in for eyes, of men with rows of caraway comfits up their vests for buttons; there were hearts too, and leaf shapes.[2]

Of all the Christmas pastries, the gingerbread cookie was the one most loved by early American children. I suspect that a large part of this popularity hinged on the fact that

The Christmas Cook

Cookie made with an eighteenth-century wooden mold. See the 1833 Gingerbread recipe on PAGE 124.

gingerbread was cheap, easy to make, a small batch would yield many cookies, and that gingerbread dough stood up fairly well under the vagaries of both brick-oven and cook-stove baking. It was pretty difficult to ruin it, and one only needed a sensitive nose to know the precise moment when it was done. Of course, there was a clamoring minority by the 1870s that declared no baking would be possible without a thermometer: "Perhaps the day will come when housewives will learn to regulate their ovens with a thermometer, till then we wonder how anybody can possibly tell the 'exact degree of heat'

required for anything: as if your fire depended entirely upon the kind of wood you burn, the number of lumps of coal you use, or the side up either are put into the stove."[3]

Well, that is exactly how it worked. And now that we do have oven thermometers, we are still guessing—what oven is less than 50°F off from the setting on the dial? And what oven does not have its hot corner, bakes "fast" at one temperature or too slow at another? It would be wise to purchase *two* ovenproof thermometers and test different parts of your oven at different readings. At this juncture in the book, this advice may seem like an afterthought, but with cookies, it is an especially crucial and timely reminder. There are some recipes at the end of this chapter that are precise in their timing, provided that the temperature is accurate— 1 minute too much and they are ruined.

In American cookery, there are two distinct families of gingerbread cookies, the honey-based gingerbreads of Middle European origin—mostly Germany—and the molasses shortbreads that developed in England or Scotland, depending on which historian you wish to believe. The honey-based gingerbreads are the oldest, tracing to classical antiquity. The other developed in the late seventeenth century, using molasses as a substitute for honey. This in turn required adjustments in the proportions of flour and other ingredients.

Some pinpoint the shift to molasses after England acquired Jamaica in 1664. Once England gained Jamaica, sugar cane became a

Beware of Camels

colonial product rather than a taxable import. Since molasses was produced in large quantities, it was always cheaper than honey, particularly in early America. You will find molasses in Crisp Ginger Cake on page 147, a prototype for many of our modern gingersnap recipes. However, once you read the recipe for Brandy Snaps on page 137, you will understand why *gingersnap* is such a misnomer. Old-style snaps were a species of lace cookie, not a form of gingerbread.

The Germans in this country were the best honey cake bakers—they called the cookies *Lebkuchen,* a name itself with very ancient and much disputed meanings among linguists. Personally, I side with the faction that believes *Leb-* stems from *Cleb-,* the Germanized form of *clebanus,* a small portable oven.[4] The Romans baked their gingerbreads in small, portable ovens, and so did the gingerbread bakers in the Middle Ages. I never thought that was too difficult to figure out, but there *are* linguists who do not cook.

Off and on under various emperors during the early Christian era, Trier (Augusta Trevirorum) became the capital of the Roman Empire. It also became a center for gingerbread baking. By the late Middle Ages, this primacy had long since faded, and gingerbread baking had shifted to such centers as Aachen, Nürnberg, and Ulm. Nürnberg has maintained an international reputation in this field even to this day.

In America, the German Lebkuchen tradition was continued in Pennsylvania among the Pennsylvania Dutch, but also in the large German neighborhoods in New York, Baltimore, Cincinnati, Dayton, and Milwaukee. The secret to good gingerbread, as all these German bakers knew, was spelt flour.[5] *Triticum speltum,* a coarse form of wheat, yields a starchy flour that when mixed with rye produces an absolutely perfect base for gingerbread. Spelts were also used in making flour for pretzels.

I had great trepidation in choosing a Lebkuchen recipe for this book because the classic recipes usually demand highly detailed and time-consuming preparation techniques in addition to the special flour mix. However, I found the answer to this problem in a rare New York cookbook from 1859. The

Clebanus or portable oven. From a 1483 German woodcut.

recipe can be made with common pastry flour and the results are truly wonderful, one of my favorite cookies in this entire book. You will find the recipe near the end of this chapter.

Some Lebkuchen rise very little during baking, and those recipes are ideal for stamping with wooden molds. Others puff and are best iced or eaten plain. It may come as no surprise to the rest of the country that the Pennsylvania Dutch take this matter very seriously. But I do think it is amusing that in the 1950s a huge controversy broke out in the Lehigh Valley (near Allentown) over the issue of whether Christmas Lebkuchen— and Christmas cookies in general—should be iced or not.

The first salvo came from the Allentown *Sunday Call-Chronicle,* and the battle raged back and forth in the columns of that newspaper for three years running.[6] As one editor put it, it developed into a veritable pitched battle of sample cookies, all of which he had the diplomatic if not infinitely pleasant task of tasting. The issue, incidentally, was never settled.

If the parties to that infamous cookie war had only known the truth, they would have stopped in their tracks before their ovens. Gingerbread was often treated like marzipan, particularly stamped gingerbread, because like marzipan, it was easy to gild. If gold leaf seems a bit garish to our present standards of taste (not to mention pocketbooks), years ago it was considered quite festive, the end of all ends for gingerbread. Just keep in mind

that we still wrap fancy chocolates in foils. So common was gilt gingerbread in fact that *The Family Receipt Book* (Pittsburgh, 1819) included a little remedy for it under "The Danger of Children Eating Gilt Gingerbread."[7] Many marzipan and sugarwork figures were actually covered with fake gilding in the form of copper foil, which was even deadlier to swallow.

Since Christmas foods were intended in part for children—particularly the confections and pastries—certain themes do appear repeatedly, especially as pictorial motifs. Albert Walzer and other historians of carved wooden molds have dealt rather extensively with European iconography, that is, with the meaning of the pictures, but no comparable study is available on the American side.[8] Generally speaking, there is a fairly close relationship between popular prints and pictorial cakes or pastries. Carvers were often aware of the heavy symbolic themes expressed, and in some cases, they adapted their work directly from period prints or engravings.

The caveat, however, is that one cannot necessarily date a Springerle mold or a tin cookie cutter by its picture. Collectors often overlook this crucial point. Because Christmas is traditional, and by that I mean backward-looking, many images remained in use for a very long time. Ladies in eighteenth-century dresses were as popular in the nineteenth century as the fairy tales in which they appeared. However, once commercialization entered the picture, dating of objects became easier and more closely tied to yearly trends in professional literature.

The flood of cheap imported wares from Germany between 1871 and 1906 when the import laws were changed, inundated our Christmas markets with cooking utensils like the cookie cutters below. Unlike homemade counterparts, or local tinsmith's wares, these tools depicted highly stylized images, often drawn from secular themes or, as in this case, with subjects designed specially to hang on the Christmas tree. Likewise, recipes ap-

Circular tin cookie cutter for North German Christmas Cookies (PAGE 131), circa 1915. In the foreground, a crimped cookie cutter from about 1885 and the decorated cookie that it makes.

peared in popular cookbooks to better match the demands of such utensils—the North German Christmas Cookies are a perfect example, but so too are the Nic-Nacs and the Yule Dollies already mentioned in chapter 1. In a sense, with the advent of inexpensive tin cutters, new emphasis was placed on *shape,* where in the past, many homemade cookies simply had been square or round. Bells, Christmas trees, camels, crimped wares (cutters with zigzag edges), lilies, Santa Clauses, turkeys, all of these elaborate shapes tended to deemphasize texture and flavor. In the case of the commercial Yule Dollies, the vanilla-flavored cookie (not bad by itself) was virtually buried beneath the icing required to create the visual effect of a doll in a peasant dress.

Regardless, by the turn of this century Yule Dollies had become immensely popular, promoted in no small measure by large urban bakeries. The Anger Baking Company of New York, for example, illustrated an elaborately decorated version of the dolly (complete with a real feather in her cap!) in *The Confectioners' Journal* of September 1899.[9] I have modeled my reconstruction after that photograph. As in the original, her face is done with a scrap picture.

For all the evocations of ancient yule dows and the harmless fun Victorian bakers had with it, the dolly theme was sometimes viewed suspiciously by conservative American religious groups who demanded symbols less *foreign* and centering on more "Christian" iconography. In J. H. Kuhlman's *Holi-*

The Christmas Cook

Yule Dollie iced according to an 1899 advertisement in *The Confectioners' Journal.* Yule Dollie cookie cutter, circa 1895. (Philadelphia Museum of Art)

day Help: New Ideas for Christmas for Sunday Schools and Day Schools (Loudonville, Ohio, 1917), Yule Dollies were patriotically depaganized and transformed into Dolly Angels.[10] Such image conversion was common in American Protestantism—fully missing the fact that the primary form of the English medieval yule dow was the Baby Cake, an image of the Christ Child.

The human figure is an old, old motif in Christmas cookery, as even a cursory glance at European gingerbread mold collections will reveal. This should not be surprising, since Adam and Eve Day fell on December 24. The duality of male and female figures based on this theme is repeated over and over again in Christmas iconography, with Mary gradually assuming the role of Eve and

Hänsel and Gretel cookie cutters from the 1890s, also sold as Hans Brinker sets. In front of them, a parody of the Hänsel and Gretel motif: a gingerbread witch riding a goat.

Christ the New Adam.[11] In Protestant literature, the Christmas tree assumes the role of the Tree of Life.

Folk culture often produced comic parodies of these themes, best illustrated perhaps in the Swiss Springerle cookie (page 55) showing a man and woman shaking down the Tree of Life for babies, which the woman is catching in her apron. The sexual implications were not lost, not even on the children for whom these cookies were originally made. American parodies on this theme, influenced by popular culture, would include such subjects as the Hänsel and Gretel sets manufactured by James Y. Watkins of New York. They were later marketed as Hans Brinker sets when that children's book became a best-seller.[12]

The nineteenth-century moralists were not amused by religious parodies—especially in connection with Christmas. Do not forget that Hänsel and Gretel baked a witch into gingerbread. That culinary triumph of good over evil vindicated the old themes of Protestant morality so prevalent in earlier Christmas iconography.

In some areas of this country, these themes were repeated in local tradition, as in the case of the "Tillie" sets made by Pennsylvania German tinsmiths. These sets depict characters from the 1904 satiric novel *Tillie, A Mennonite Maid*.[13] Today, they have been replaced by Amish figures.

If we step back from nineteenth-century America into European Christmases of the seventeenth century, the range of pastry

The Christmas Cook

types gradually narrows, until we reach the Middle Ages, when a large proportion of the most traditional Christmas foods was consumed almost exclusively by the noble or urban upper classes. Jumbles, kringles, bagels, doughnuts, and pretzels all ultimately share the same genealogical tree, and thus belong to this category of Christmas food. Jumbles, called *Butter-Kringeln* in north Germany, were not available to all people because of the expensive ingredients needed to make them: best wheat flour, eggs, sugar, and butter.[14] The same could be said of sand tarts, sugar pretzels, and a host of other baked goods now generally consumed by all levels of society.

By coming to America, most settlers were able to enjoy a qualitative improvement in their material lives. This translated very often into choice of food as symbols of well-being. There is a tendency, still very strong among many ethnic groups in this country, to prepare for everyday consumption foods that in the old country were only made at Christmas or weddings. In addition, the industrialization of food production between 1850 and 1880 made many former luxury foods available at an affordable cost, but the hidden price for this was a parallel decline in culinary craftsmanship. Jumbles are a typical example.

In eighteenth-century Anglo-American culture, Christmas jumbles were generally perceived as circular, in their basic form, a ring—for the home cook, a ring is by far the easiest to make. The name implied shape, not

a particular flavor or texture; a jumble was any kind of cookie twisted into rings, knots, or even bows. Most Christmas jumbles were baked in the shape of puffy rings; they were sometimes decorated with colored sugar—usually red—sometimes with caraway seeds, but mostly they were plain. In the case of Sugar Jumbles on page 151, a thin coating of sugar is baked into the surface of the dough to create a glaze. Incidentally, this recipe comes from the Hudson Valley, and one can see an obvious parallel in sugar-glazed doughnuts.

As sugar became cheaper in the nineteenth century, cookies in general became increasingly sweeter, especially in England and the United States, and the number of recipes

Tin cutter depicting Tillie the Mennonite Maid, circa 1904–1910.

Chromolithograph Christmas cards, circa 1885.
(Roughwood Collection)

A merry Christmas to you

in which sugar outweighed flour grew dramatically. In the case of jumbles, they evolve into a flatter and flatter profile, until the dough can no longer be handled unless kept on ice, as in the case of Carrie Lockwood's Wafer Jumbles of 1867 (page 152).

Inexpensive, mass-produced tin jumble cutters made it easier to cut soft doughs— often the same cutters used for doughnuts— and the improvement of cast-iron cooking ranges made it possible to trust such delicate pastries to the oven. Two alterations, then, occurred in American jumble cookery: a change in shape and a change in structure.

Jumbles are almost extinct today. The decline of their popularity was paralleled by a rise in popularity of sand tarts, which are richer and have more sugar. It is interesting to see how jumbles grew flatter, more like thin, brittle sand tarts toward the end of the nineteenth century, as home cooks gradually became dependent on mass-produced utensils to mold and shape their food.

SCRAP PICTURES

The impulse to decorate was not extinguished by the industrialization of Christmas cookery. Artistic expression merely found other modes of outlet. If the tin cutter allowed the Christmas cook to re-create repetitiously the identical trotting horse, the identical jumping hare, the identical heart, year after year, the scrap picture liberated the surface decoration of each cookie with infinite color and variety.

Scrap pictures, which take their name from the fact that they are small scraps or pieces of paper, probably trace their origin to the medieval practice of printing religious pictures of saints or protective devices directly on edible wafers with ink and wood blocks. These wafers, usually made at monasteries or places of religious pilgrimage, were sold or rewarded to the faithful who came for a particular cure or blessing, much in the same manner as the small *Andachtsbilder* (devotional pictures) that were printed on paper. The pictorial wafers were intended to be eaten in order to ingest (and therefore benefit from) the blessing. The *Andachtsbilder* were taken home and tucked away in a safe place with other religious artifacts. Sometimes *Andachtsbilder* were used as scraps on Christmas cookies, as in the case of the Madonna and Child on the opposite page. This picture was printed at Einsiedeln in Switzerland and widely distributed in the United States among the German immigrant community during the 1860s.[15]

The Madonna and Child is one of the oldest and most persistent decorative motifs in German-American Christmas cookery. In the sketchbooks of John Lewis Krimmel (1819–1820) at the Henry Francis DuPont Winterthur Museum in Delaware, there is a scene of a family standing around a small Christmas tree set up on a table. Over the mantel hangs a portrait of the Madonna and

Child, and on the tree itself is a large, round Springerle cookie impressed with nearly the same image.[16] This family remains unidentified in the Krimmel manuscript, but we may safely conclude that it is German Catholic, because such images would rarely have appeared in a Protestant house.

The small *Andachtsbilder* and, more important, its secular counterpart, the scrap picture, eventually served as a replacement of the molded or printed picture-cookie, especially as the craft of mold carving declined in the nineteenth century. Steam printing accelerated this process, and with the development of chromolithography (color printing from engraved stones) in the 1870s, Germany became the center for printing scrap pictures. Because they were inexpensive, German scrap pictures became a popular collectible for American children.

The gathering of these scrap pictures and arranging them in blank books, often augmented with illustrations cut from magazines and newspapers, led to the development of the term "scrapbook." But German printers also issued collections in the form of distinct catalogues, as for example the catalogues of *Oblaten* intended for the use of bakers—the German term for scrap pictures and wafers is the same. Littauer & Boysen of Berlin, Otto Maeckel of Bürgstädt (Saxony), and O. S. Heineck of Dresden all issued collections of this kind.[17] But in practice, almost any scrap picture was a candidate for use on gingerbread cookies.

The *Pictorial Scrap Book*, published at Philadelphia in 1860, is one of the earliest American commercial scrapbooks issued exclusively for Christmas. This collection is a miscellany of woodcuts meant to be painted in coloring-book fashion, cut up, and used as Christmas tree decorations. Like the squirrel shown on page 117, the scraps could be attached to blank gingerbread cookies. Or, like the auricula in the flowerpot, shown on page 143, the scrap picture itself might serve as a

Andachtsbild of the Madonna and Child from Einsiedeln, Switzerland, circa 1865. (Roughwood Collection)

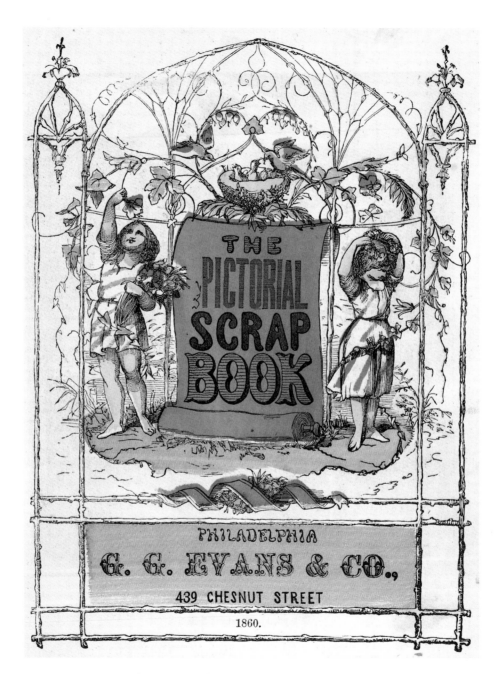

Title page of *The Pictorial Scrap Book* (1860). (Roughwood Collection)

Gilded scrap borders for gingerbread cookies, circa 1870. (Roughwood Collection)

Obviously, scraps could also be combined with molded surfaces to create dramatic decorative effects. Yet this kind of labor-intensive ornamentation required not only special baking skills, but also patience, and not every home cook had her share of both. In general, the scrap picture replaced fussy icings and printed cookies, not to the extent that iced cookies or stamped gingerbreads became extinct, but the scrap picture served as a kind of lowest common denominator. And its popularity went hand in hand with the tin model for artistic expression in such homemade cooking tools as the chocolate mold shown in chapter 3. Such potted flowers were a popular theme in Christmas tree decoration in the 1860s. They are mentioned in William Taylor's advertisement on page 61.

Lest we imagine that the age of gilding gingerbread had passed with the coming of chromolithography and scraps, the unused sheet of gold frames, stars, and other gilt scrap garnishes above should prove the contrary. A cookie on the back cover shows how such giltwork would look when used to accent a scrap picture of an Italian peasant girl.

Père Noël (Father Christmas) is portrayed as St. Nicholas in this chromolithograph scrap picture from Strasbourg, Alsace, circa 1895–1898. (Roughwood Collection)

Beware of Camels

cookie cutter. Perhaps this is best illustrated by the *Horse and Rider,* an ancient motif in Christmas cookery. In pre-Christian Europe, it was the symbol of Wotan, the supreme god of the ancient Teutons, or even more anciently, of Lugh, one of the major dieties of the Celts.

For medieval counterparts, one could point to the *Haymonskinder* cycle of folk tales (four boys riding a horse), St. George mounted on horseback as he slays the dragon—a subject of the Christmas mumming plays—or Saint Nicholas on his mule. All of these themes depict figures riding, figures raised above the common mass of humanity, figures made noble by virtue of their height. The *Haymonskinder* are a parody, since four on a horse creates its own lively comedy. But Saint Nicholas's mule is an inescapable allusion to Christ riding into Jerusalem. Thus, there are many levels of meaning to this motif.

After the Reformation, Dutch and German bakers were quick to draw upon newer Protestant images based on the horse and rider theme, among them Stadhouder Willem III of the House of Orange, and later, Frederick the Great.[18]

Both are replaced in American iconography by equestrian figures of George Washington (also Protestant, also triumphant) with sword raised. Since the craft of mold carving was not a required part of baking apprenticeship in America (as it was in Germany and Holland, for example), American bakers relied more heavily on tin forms.

These figures were then iced meticulously for window display and eventual sale.

With the rise in popularity of Santa Claus in the 1840s and 1850s—he is often called Kriss Kringle in period literature—the image of Saint Nicholas on his mule became extraordinarily common. Scrap pictures of the goodly saint allowed bakers to save time and costs in decoration. Imagine how tedious it would have been to re-create the scrap picture on page 115 in colored icings. Not only does the saint have gilded apples and pears in the basket by his leg, he is carrying in front of him a smaller basket containing sugar pretzels, jumbles, and cinnamon stars. Here is a rare instance where the decoration of one food makes direct reference to other foods sharing a Christmas context. Yet while this scrap picture has indeed taken the place of icing, it certainly goes far in fortifying many older, traditional food images.

Scrap pictures, themselves inedible, were attached to cookies with a "glue" made of sugar. This made their removal a relatively simple task; they *had* to come off before the cookie could be eaten. But large, elaborate scrap pictures were often so beautiful that some people preferred to leave them on the cookies and preserve them from Christmas to Christmas, particularly as decorations for the tree.

Scrap pictures decorate a Yule Dollie, Honey Cakes, and North German Christmas Cookies. The squirrel (LEFT) is from *The Pictorial Scrap Book* (1860). The Saint Nicholas and mule scrap picture was printed by A. & C. Kaufmann of Berlin, circa 1885.

The Christmas Cook

There were many Christmas cooks however who viewed scrap pictures as a bother. Certainly, if the pictures did not pull off, this rendered at least part of the cookie inedible. Cost was another factor; some families simply did not go to great expense at Christmas, and cooks found other ways to make their handiwork enticing. Creating a texture was one simple alternative, and this could be accomplished with many everyday tools in the kitchen.

For example, a waffle effect could be created with an oatcake roller or a meat tenderizer. A tin vegetable grater could be rolled slowly over the dough to create a pitted pattern. Butter prints came in handy not only for stamping New Years Cakes, but for gingerbreads, speculatius, and shortbreads.

The art of impressing pictures into pastry is probably one of the most mysterious branches of baking for those who have never done it. This fascination is evident in the antiques market, where some American New Years cake boards now realize many thousands of dollars. New Years Cake is the early American equivalent of Springerle, although, in the hands of American cooks, the structure of the original Dutch recipes often underwent radical alteration. Mrs. Timothy Dwight's Cookies and the recipe for Christmas Cookies from *New American Cookery* (1805) show clear evidence of this. They are also early examples of the assimilation into English of the term *koekje* (little cake) from New Netherlands Dutch. Sometime in the

The basket of fruit, a symbol of plenty and prosperity, was used to make the Gingerbread cookie on PAGE XVI. All three molds shown here are American and date from about 1810–1820.

latter part of the eighteenth century, *koekje* became the American word *cookie*.[19]

In her *Directions for Cookery* of 1837, Eliza Leslie published an excellent recipe for New Years cakes and mentioned the wooden prints used to stamp them. The prints she referred to were small, like the one illustrated on page 141. That mold is believed to have belonged to her; it bears her initials and an ownership number.

The Christmas Cook

Small wooden prints were more typical of home cookery than the large one used to make the New Years Cake on page 63. Even the level of execution of the small molds reflects their homey context, as in the examples shown on the opposite page.

Many popular themes converge in these molds, such as the basket of fruit, a variation of the cornucopia, itself an image drawn from classical religions. The fruit in these baskets was often gilded, in reference to the basket of gilded fruit carried by Saint Nicholas shown in the scrap picture on page 115.

Contrary to popular belief, very few Pennsylvania German Springerle boards were actually carved in this country, since there was an active Christmas trade with the Old World throughout the eighteenth and nineteenth centuries. Even Nürnberg gingerbreads were imported directly.[20] On the other hand, small New Years Cake prints worked as readily on Springerle dough as on New Years Cake dough, and the baking technique for both was actually the same. Bakeries sold New Years Cake boards for essentially both purposes.

Many German settlers brought heirloom molds with them, as in the case of the dated 1843 Springerle board shown at right. It is masterfully carved and resembles the work of a school of Springerle carvers in Swabia in the presentday German state of Baden-Württemberg.[21]

American craftsmen could never fully compete against the inexpensively produced and often higher quality wares imported from Germany during the nineteenth century. There was no guild system to require a mastery of mold carving and good carvers were simply in too short a supply.

George Endriss of Philadelphia skirted the shortage of competent carvers by casting

Springerle board brought to America by immigrants from Swabia in present Baden-Württemberg, dated 1843. (Philadelphia Museum of Art)

Beware of Camels

Springerle boards in pewter. Herman Hueg of Long Island City, New York, also engaged in this trade. Pewter Springerle boards mimic the earlier concept of carving Springerle boards in earthenware or tile, except that with pewter, one carver could create the master mold from which all others were cast.

Interesting as they may be, the pewter Springerle boards are not in the same category of craftsmanship as the Swabian board discussed earlier. In fact, the masters from which the Endriss boards were cast were machine carved. Artistic deficiencies aside, the metal Springerle boards acquired a certain following, especially in small family bakeries. As an advertisement in 1926 pointed out, metal cake prints eliminated problems with sticky dough. This was accomplished by keeping the cake print cold.[22] Metal Springerle boards are still sold today by Pfeil and Holing of New York. Their boards are made of cast aluminum.

In a sense, mass-produced utensils introduced decorative treatments of their own. Crimped wares, that is, cookie cutters with elaborate zigzag borders, became available in the 1870s, and by the 1880s, they were cheap enough to appear in standard cookbook literature. The woodcut above is reproduced from *Practical Housekeeping* (Minneapolis, 1884) under the heading "Kitchen Luxuries."[23] Obviously, not everyone could afford them.

The interior patterns of these cutters were intended to mark the doughs with lines so

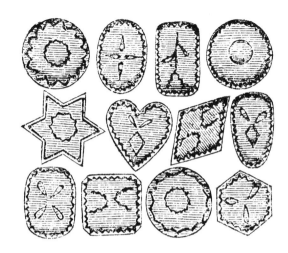

Crimped tin cookie cutters from *Practical Housekeeping* (1884). (Roughwood Collection)

that unsteady (or uncreative) hands would have no trouble in guessing where the icing should go, thus reducing the Christmas cook to a less efficient version of a mechanical bakery. The guesswork was also eliminated for professional bakers, who could consult such trade manuals as Josef Angerer's *Der moderne Konditor* (The Modern Confectioner), which illustrated with color plates precisely how to decorate each type of Christmas cookie. I have iced several cookies shown on page 100 based on Angerer designs.

Since the turn of this century, the craft of cookie baking, especially in this country, has undergone a radical shift both in recipe structure and in style of presentation. Exaggerated portions and a coarse, "rustic" ap-

The Christmas Cook

pearance designed to imply a homemade look have replaced the small, delicate pastries of the type illustrated in my introduction and elsewhere in this book. The gilded, feather-edged cookies shown beside the Wafers and Jelly on page 27 look machine made even though they were formed by hand one at a time with a mold dating from the eighteenth century. The economics of such labor-intensive work have relegated this type of pastry to the museum, or at best to the lucky few whose friends are willing once a year to bake such dainty surprises for gift baskets and Christmas stockings.

Creative expression, that cutting edge which kept us ahead of our competitors in Europe and Asia, has oftentimes been checkmated by an old Yankee presumption that shortcuts are best. In essence, what is cheap or free is better than what we might create ourselves. Manufacturers of consumer baking products often contribute to this inadvertently. Their promotional cookbooks not only introduce new recipes and new foods—new but not necessarily better—but sometimes include little perks for their customers in the form of cookie cutters like the one shown in the advertisement on page 122 for Dromedary Cocoanut.[24] Incidentally, you may note that the dromedary cookie cutter is in fact not a dromedary but a camel; it does not have two humps.

The camel and dromedary certainly provide us with an excellent example of how commercialization introduces new imagery to the Christmas setting. In the eighteenth century, camels were not a widely used motif in connection with this holiday, at least not in the United States. They were definitely viewed as exotic, the association being more with the Arab world than with the Christian. The commercialization of Christmas in the nineteenth century, and, in particular, the commercial adaptations of the Three Wise Men in Christmas card iconography at the turn of this century, greatly changed this. So much so that a Christmas association immediately springs to mind today when we see camel or dromedary cookie cutters.

The camel was also a product logo for several canned foods in the Victorian period, the point being that such foods as the Dromedary brand desiccated coconut would keep for a long time, just as camels survive the dessert. This is not Christmas iconography, but the similarity certainly contributes to an advantageous intermingling of imagery. The Christmas story has thus grown by virtue of such accretions.

Beware of Camels

Advertisement from 1915 for a camel "dromedary"
cookie cutter. (Roughwood Collection)

COCONUT DROMEDARIES

1902

*I*f coconut dromedaries could walk, they would certainly make the most delectable of desserts "on the hoof"! The citizens of Puerto Rico need no reminder about the importance of camels or dromedaries to their own unique celebration of Christmas, a celebration that today has spilled over into New York's Spanish Harlem and other places where Puerto Ricans have settled. On Twelfth Night, which they call Three Kings Day, camels, not Santa Claus, deliver presents and goodies to the children. Straw is set out the night before to insure that the camel has plenty to eat and won't forget to come back next year. For apartment dwellers without fireplaces, there is always the annual difficulty of explaining to the little ones how it is Santa Claus will ever get into the living room on Christmas Eve. But imagine the complicated strategies my Puerto Rican acquaintances use to explain how it is that under the cover of darkness camels can dart like cats up fire escapes to a fifteenth floor flat!

YIELD: APPROXIMATELY 3 DOZEN COOKIES.

½ pound (2 sticks) unsalted butter
1 cup sugar
3 eggs
3 tablespoons milk
2 teaspoons vanilla extract
5 cups all-purpose flour
1 teaspoon baking powder
1 cup grated coconut

*C*ream together the butter and sugar. Beat the eggs to a froth, add the milk and vanilla, then combine with the butter mixture. Sift the flour and baking powder twice, then sift 4 cups into the batter. Add the coconut, and, finally, the last cup of flour. Work this into a dough just soft enough that it does not stick to the hands. Cover and set in the refrigerator to ripen overnight.

Preheat the oven to 350°F.

Flour the work surface and roll out the dough ¼ inch thick. Cut into camels or dromedaries and bake on greased baking sheets in the preheated oven for 15 minutes. Cool on racks.

NOTE: The cookies may be further decorated by brushing them with a mixture of milk and sugar and then covering them with finely grated coconut to given them a furry appearance, like the camel shown on page 100. Rabbits may be made in the same manner for Easter.

SOURCE: Annie R. Gregory, *Woman's Favorite Cook Book* (Chicago: Sold by subscription, 1902), 252.

GINGERBREAD
— 1833 —

YIELD: APPROXIMATELY 8 DOZEN 2-INCH COOKIES.

1 pound unsalted butter	*2 tablespoons ground ginger*
½ cup brown sugar	*1½ teaspoons ground cloves*
1 cup unsulfured molasses	*1½ teaspoons ground mace*
1 egg	*1½ teaspoons grated nutmeg*
6 cups all-purpose flour	*1 tablespoon ground coriander*
¾ cup rye flour (see note)	*1 tablespoon caraway seeds*

Heat the butter, sugar, and molasses in a saucepan until the butter is melted and the sugar completely dissolved. Let cool slightly.

Beat the egg. Sift the flour and spices together twice and make a hole in the center. Add the beaten egg, the molasses mixture, and the caraway seeds. Stir to form a stiff dough. Cover and set in the refrigerator at least 3 days—or as long as 1 month.

Preheat the oven to 350°F.

Roll out the dough ¼ inch thick and cut into 2-inch rounds or whatever shapes you choose. Set the cookies on greased baking sheets and bake in the preheated oven 8 to 10 minutes. Cool on racks.

NOTE: Some grades of rye flour contain large pieces of bran. Be certain that the rye flour you use for this recipe is free of these bran flakes; otherwise, sift them out yourself.

SOURCE: *The Family's Guide* (Cortland, N.Y.: C. W. Mason, 1833), 6.

Various Springerle cookies reflect changing fashions in Christmas themes, from the nativity scene made with a mold dated 1642, and the diamond-shaped picture of boys playing games, circa 1790, to the 1870s cameos (TOP LEFT) and the Buckeye leaf cookie from a Dayton, Ohio mold, circa 1885.

SWEET PRETZELS

1914

Pretzels are historically one of the oldest decorations for the Christmas tree. Sweet or Sugar Pretzels are particularly attractive because of their snowy appearance when tucked into the evergreens. They can be seen around the base of the apple pyramid on page 50.

YIELD: APPROXIMATELY 5 DOZEN SMALL PRETZELS.

½ pound (2 sticks) unsalted butter
1 cup sugar
1 egg
½ teaspoon almond extract
3 cups pastry flour
2 tablespoons rosewater

Cream the butter and sugar. Beat the egg to a froth then combine with the sugar mixture. Add the extract. Gradually sift in the flour; if the dough becomes too dry, moisten it with the rosewater. However, the dough should be relatively stiff. Form into a ball, cover, and refrigerate overnight.

Preheat the oven to 375°F.

Break the dough into 50 to 60 equal pieces and roll them out to about 8 inches in length. Twist into pretzel shapes and set them on greased baking sheets. Bake in the preheated oven 12 to 15 minutes, or until golden brown on the bottom. Cool on racks.

NOTE: Ovens that bake hot should be set at 350°F, since this dough burns easily; baking time would be approximately 18 minutes.

After they are baked, you may brush the pretzels with a mixture of water, egg white, and sugar, then dip them in *Hagelzucker* (hail sugar), which resembles the coarse salt on common pretzels. *Hagelzucker* is made in Germany and is available from some specialty shops in this country.

SOURCE: Mrs. C. E. Dietrich, *Family Cook Book of German Recipes* (Richmond, Va.: A. S. Kratz Co., 1914), 35.

YULE DOLLIES

YIELD: 1 TO 2 DOZEN 5-INCH DOLLS.

8 tablespoons (1 stick) unsalted butter
1 cup sugar
2 eggs
1 tablespoon heavy cream

1 teaspoon vanilla extract
3 cups all-purpose flour
2 teaspoons baking powder

Cream the butter and sugar. Beat the eggs to a froth and combine with the sugar mixture. Add the cream and vanilla. Sift the flour and baking powder together twice, then sift into the batter. Work this into a dough, cover, and rest it in the refrigerator for 1 hour before baking.

Preheat the oven to 350°F.

Roll out the dough to about ½ inch thick and cut out the dollies with a tin cutter. Set them on greased baking sheets and bake in the preheated oven for 15 minutes. Cool on racks. Ice and decorate like the dolly shown on page 107.

SOURCE: Recipe of Cornelia C. Bedford, *Table Talk* 14 (November 1899), 435.

ROYAL ICING FOR YULE DOLLIES

YIELD: 2½ CUPS

3½ cups (1 pound) confectioners' sugar
2 egg whites

1 teaspoon lemon juice
Food coloring (to taste)

Sift the sugar to remove the lumps. Beat the egg whites until frothy, then gradually combine with the sugar. Beat until it stands in peaks, then add the lemon juice and coloring. Apply to the cookies with a stiff brush or small knife.

LITTLE PLUMCAKES

1810

This tasty cookie is one of the prototypes of the modern drop cookie. Unlike many cookies, this one is also very good served hot. It is excellent with ice cream, and when iced makes an ornamental accent in displays of cookies like those shown on page 214.

YIELD: 4 DOZEN COOKIES.

12 tablespoons (1½ sticks) unsalted butter
¾ cup superfine sugar
3 eggs

3½ cups pastry flour
1 teaspoon grated nutmeg
½ teaspoon ground cloves
1⅔ cups currants

Preheat the oven to 375°F.

Cream the butter and sugar. Beat the eggs to a thick froth and combine with the sugar mixture. Sift the flour and spices together twice. Fold the currants into the batter, then sift in the flour. Thoroughly work the ingredients together to make a very stiff dough. Break off pieces and roll them into balls the size of walnuts. Set these on baking sheets lined with baking parchment. Bake in the preheated oven for approximately 15 minutes, or until golden brown on the bottom. Cool on racks or serve immediately.

SOURCE: Maria Rundell. *A New System of Domestic Cookery* (Philadelphia: Benjamin C. Buzby, 1810), 198.

Chromolithograph trade card, circa 1880. (Roughwood Collection)

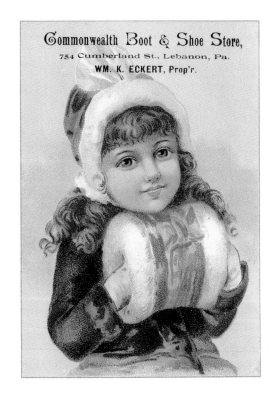

Commonwealth Boot & Shoe Store,
754 Cumberland St., Lebanon, Pa.
WM. K. ECKERT, Prop'r.

MRS. TIMOTHY DWIGHT'S COOKIES

1795

Mrs. Dwight was the wife of the first President of Yale University. She left Greenfield Hill, Connecticut, in 1795 to go to New Haven with her husband. Evidently, prior to leaving, she passed this recipe along to a friend. It was finally published in 1899 by the Village Improvement Society of Greenfield Hill.

This is nearly but not the same as the cookie called "Apeas" in Philadelphia—without rosewater and lemon, which I mentioned under the recipe for Chocolate Apeas. It is puzzling that in lower New England, Apeas were referred to as *cookies* even though the recipe itself had no early connection with New Netherlands. Usually, the early recipes that go by the name of cookie also have a Dutch origin, as in the case of the recipe from Amelia Simmons and the 1805 recipe for Christmas Cookies. Mrs. Dwight's recipe, therefore, is evidence of a shift in the term away from strictly Dutch recipes to a more general application.

The pearlash required in the original recipe has been adjusted to baking powder. Pearlash was a chemical leavener made from refined potash, a salt made from lye.

YIELD: APPROXIMATELY 3 DOZEN 3-INCH COOKIES.

10 tablespoons unsalted butter
1¼ cup superfine sugar
1 egg
1 cup milk

5½ cups all-purpose flour
1½ teaspoons baking powder
1 tablespoon caraway seeds

Cream the butter and sugar. Beat the egg and milk to a froth, then combine with the butter mixture. Sift the flour and baking powder together twice; gradually sift into the batter, beating gently and adding caraway seeds until a soft dough is formed. Cover and refrigerate overnight.

Preheat the oven to 350°F.

Roll out the dough ½ inch thick and cut into 3-inch cookies. Set these on greased baking sheets and bake in the preheated oven 10 to 15 minutes, or until golden brown on the bottom. Cool on racks.

SOURCE: Village Improvement Society of Greenfield Hill, *The Book for the Cook* (Bridgeport, Conn.: The Hurd & Taylor Co., 1899), 81.

Nic-Nacs

1877

According to an article in *Bakers' Helper* for January 1898, Nic-Nacs were an inexpensive version of the English Cornhill biscuit.[26] They were called Nic-Nacs simply to distinguish them from real Cornhills.

James Parkinson (page 1) mentions Nic-Nacs among the feast of Christmas goodies enjoyed by American children each year. Because they are a form of shortbread, Nic-Nacs mold very easily into a great variety of fancy shapes.

YIELD: APPROXIMATELY 8 DOZEN 2-INCH COOKIES.

○

½ cup superfine sugar
1 pound (4 sticks) unsalted butter

4 cups pastry flour

○

Rub the sugar and butter into the flour using a coarse sieve. Form into a soft dough and ripen in the refrigerator overnight.

Preheat the oven to 325°F and prepare the glaze for the cookies.

Glaze for Nic-Nacs

1 egg   *¼ cup milk, at room temperature*

○

Beat the egg to a cream and set aside. Roll out the dough to ¼ inch thick and cut into desired shapes. Set these on baking sheets lined with baking parchment and brush each Nic-Nac with milk. Bake 17 minutes in the preheated oven; remove and brush with the beaten egg. Brush each cookie twice. Return the Nic-Nacs to the oven and bake an additional 5 minutes or until the glaze turns golden. Cool on racks and store in airtight containers.

SOURCE: *The Confectioners' Journal* 3 (August 1877), 17.

—— 1905 ——

I shall quote the original recipe: "This recipe will make a large quantity, and they are pretty to hang upon the tree during Christmas week, and to pass in baskets to holiday callers. This is the *bona fide* Christmas cookie."[27]

This recipe was also illustrated with a woodcut of a collection of commercial tin cutters, some of which are shown on page 106. I am not certain what makes this "North German," but I can tell you that this dough will work in Speculatius molds. Baking time will depend on the size and thickness of the cookie you make. It is advisable to bake large Speculatius figures (some are over 3 feet high) on baking parchment. This helps greatly in moving them on and off the baking sheet.

YIELD: APPROXIMATELY 6 DOZEN 2-INCH COOKIES.

¾ cup unsulfured molasses
1 cup sugar
½ pound (2 sticks) unsalted butter
5½ cups all-purpose flour
¼ teaspoon baking soda
1 tablespoon ground cloves

1½ tablespoons ground cinnamon
⅓ cup chopped citron
1 tablespoon rosewater or arrack
(see note)
1½ tablespoons aniseed

Warm the molasses, sugar, and butter in a saucepan until the butter melts and the sugar is completely dissolved. Sift the flour, baking soda, and spices twice. Put the flour in a large work bowl, make a hole in the center, and add the warm butter mixture. Add the chopped citron and rosewater or arrack. Stir and work this into a heavy dough. Cover and ripen in the refrigerator for 3 days.

Preheat the oven to 350°F.

Scatter the aniseed on the work surface and roll the dough out over this so the seeds adhere to the underside. Cut out the cookies and set them on greased baking sheets. Bake them in the preheated oven 10 to 12 minutes. Cool on racks.

NOTE: Arrack is a distilled beverage usually flavored with anise. Much of the arrack sold in this country comes from Lebanon.

SOURCE: *The Original Buckeye Cook Book* (St. Paul, Minn.: Webb Publishing Co., 1905), 83.

NEW YEARS CRACKERS

In an 1805 cookbook, *New American Cookery*, there is a recipe for New Years Cake that is a form of biscuit. It is sweet and contains caraway seeds and is leavened with yeast. This recipe, however, is not of Dutch origin; it is a true cracker and was sometimes either stamped with a print or merely pricked with a fork. Traditionally, these crackers were meant to be eaten with jams or sweetmeats and may have been among those foods that were once served in the Chesapeake Bay region to Christmas and New Years mummers.

YIELD: APPROXIMATELY 6 DOZEN 2-INCH CRACKERS.

3 cups pastry flour
½ teaspoon salt

1½ cup heavy cream

Preheat the oven to 350°F.

Put the flour, salt, and cream in a deep mixing bowl and combine to form a soft dough. Dust your work surface with flour and knead the dough until it becomes soft and pliant and snaps when pulled. The more you knead the dough the tenderer the crackers will be.

Roll out the dough as thin as possible and cut into 2-inch rounds. Stamp with a biscuit dock (to put holes in them) or prick with a fork. Bake on lightly greased baking sheets in the preheated oven for 15 minutes. Cool on racks and store in airtight containers.

SOURCE: Mrs. M. E. Porter, *Mrs. Porter's New Southern Cookery Book* (Philadelphia: John E. Potter & Co., 1871), 184–85.

New Years Cracker (CENTER) and a Nic-Nac cookie with a variety of tin cutters.

IDEAL COOKIES

1921

I chose this recipe because it is an example of the type of Christmas cookie taught in home economics schools for blacks, in this case, at Hampton Institute in Virginia. It is many light years away from the Sweet Johnny Cake, the Dandy Jack Pudding, or even Brown Betty.

At the turn of this century, the aim of Hampton Institute was to send out teachers and professional people from its ranks, and one might say that Carrie Lyford's manual was quite useful in bringing the word of home economics into kitchens where very little instruction had existed earlier. On the other hand, it is interesting to note that while the opportunity was before her, there was no effort in the book to preserve Afro-American culture in terms of foods and foodways.

YIELD: 8 DOZEN COOKIES.

8 tablespoons (1 stick) unsalted butter
2 cups sugar
2 teaspoons ground cinnamon
1 tablespoon grated nutmeg
2 eggs
½ cup milk
4½ cups all-purpose flour
2 teaspoons baking powder

Cream the butter and sugar. Add the cinnamon and nutmeg. Beat the eggs to a froth, and add them to the sugar mixture. Add the milk and beat well.

Sift the flour and baking powder together twice. Gradually sift it into the batter. Form the dough into a ball, cover, and set in the refrigerator to ripen 12 hours.

Preheat the oven to 375°F.

Dust your hands with flour and break off pieces of dough about the size of a walnut and form into balls. Set these on greased baking sheets and bake in the preheated oven for 15 minutes.

SOURCE: Carrie Alberta Lyford, *A Book of Recipes for the Cooking School* (Hampton, Va.: The Hampton Normal and Agricultural Institute, 1921), 254.

Beware of Camels

Chromolithograph Christmas cards, Germany,
circa 1910. (Roughwood Collection)

ALMOND CAKES

1900

YIELD: APPROXIMATELY 4 DOZEN 3-INCH DIAMONDS.

½ pound (2 sticks) unsalted butter
½ cup superfine sugar
4 egg yolks
3 tablespoons cream

4 cups pastry flour
1½ teaspoons ground cinnamon
1 teaspoon grated nutmeg
Confectioners' sugar

Preheat the oven to 350°F.

Cream the butter and sugar. Beat the eggs and add the cream. Sift the flour and spices together twice. Combine the sugar and egg mixtures, then sift in the flour. Work this into a soft dough. Dust the work surface with confectioners' sugar and roll out the dough ¼ inch thick. Cut into diamond shapes with a tin cutter or pie crimper, and set them on greased baking sheets. Bake in the preheated oven 8 to 12 minutes, or until light brown on the bottom. Cool on racks. While the cookies are cooling, reset the oven to 200°F and prepare the icing as follows.

ICING FOR ALMOND CAKES

2 egg yolks
2 tablespoons water
¾ cup confectioners' sugar
Almond extract or rosewater
(optional)

½ pound finely chopped
blanched almonds

Beat the egg yolks and water, then sift in the confectioners' sugar. Beat until the icing becomes thick and batterlike. If you prefer, you may at this point flavor it with almond extract or rosewater. Using a small paintbrush, ice the tops of the cookies and scatter the chopped almonds over them. Return the cookies to the oven, and dry the icing for 5 minutes.

SOURCE: *The Bethlehem Cook Book* (Bethlehem, Pa.: Times Publishing Co., 1900), 148.

BRANDY SNAPS

1893

Snaps are crisp, wafer-thin cookies that verge on hard taffy in composition, so high is the proportion of sugar in them. They are shown on page 214. You can see from that why the so-called gingersnaps sold today are not really gingersnaps at all. If you want to make real gingersnaps, just add 2 teaspoons of ground ginger to the recipe given here.

YIELD: APPROXIMATELY 4 DOZEN COOKIES.

8 tablespoons (1 stick) unsalted butter
½ cup brown sugar
1 cup unsulfured molasses
2 teaspoons brandy
¾ cup flour

Preheat the oven to 350°F.

Cream the butter and sugar and beat until very light. Add the molasses and brandy, then sift in the flour. Beat this into a thick batter that resembles stiff whipped cream.

Grease a cookie sheet and put six teaspoon scoops of batter on it, keeping them well apart because each scoop will spread to about 5 inches. Bake in the preheated oven 10 to 12 minutes. The snaps will be ready to come out of the oven when they stop bubbling violently and begin to brown along the edges. Watch them carefully toward the end of baking; a minute too long and they will burn.

Remove from the oven and let them cool a few seconds (no more than 30), then *work quickly* while the snaps are still soft. Lift them with a cake knife and drape them over an unpainted broom handle or a wine bottle to cool. Or use a glass rolling pin, as was customary years ago. Within 5 minutes the snaps will be stiff and brittle and ready to put away.

Repeat this process until all of the batter is used. The broken snaps (you will always break a few of them) may be scattered on ice cream like burnt almonds.

NOTE: If you try to do more than six at one time, the snaps are likely to run together on the baking sheet and you will have difficulty removing them. Also, use a baking sheet with upturned edges or the batter may run over into the oven.

SOURCES: *Table Talk* 8 (March 1893), 83.

SAND TARTS

YIELD: APPROXIMATELY 8 DOZEN COOKIES.

½ pound (2 sticks) unsalted butter
2½ cups sugar
1 egg
1 egg yolk

3 tablespoons lemon extract
2 teaspoons ground cinnamon
2½ cups all-purpose flour

Cream the butter and 2 cups sugar. Beat the eggs to a froth and combine with the sugar mixture. Add the lemon and cinnamon. Sift in the flour and work into a soft dough. Roll up in a ball, cover, and ripen in the refrigerator 2 to 3 hours.

Preheat the oven to 350°F.

Roll out the dough as thin as possible and cut out 2-inch rounds. Put the cookies on lightly greased baking sheets and sprinkle the remaining ½ cup sugar over them. Bake in the preheated oven for 15 minutes. Cool on racks. To maintain crispness, store in airtight containers.

SOURCE: Deborah H. Parker and Jane E. Weeden, *Indiana W.C.T.U. Hadley Industrial School Cook Book* (Indianapolis: Organizer Print, 1883), 118–19.

Chromolithograph Christmas card, Philadelphia, 1896. (Roughwood Collection)

SHELLBARK CAKES

1912

YIELD: APPROXIMATELY 5 DOZEN COOKIES.

8 tablespoons (1 stick) unsalted butter
8 tablespoons lard or shortening
2 cups sugar
4 eggs, separated
½ cup buttermilk
3 cups all-purpose flour

1 teaspoon salt
1 teaspoon cream of tartar
1 teaspoon baking soda
1 teaspoon grated nutmeg
1½ cups chopped hickory nuts

*P*reheat the oven to 375°F.

Combine the butter and lard and beat until creamy. Add the sugar and work to a crumb. Beat the egg yolks, add the buttermilk to them, and stir this into the sugar mixture. Beat until smooth and light.

Sift the flour, salt, cream of tartar, baking soda, and nutmeg twice. Sift 2 cups of the flour mixture into the batter. Beat the egg whites until stiff and fold them into the batter. Add the chopped nuts and the remaining cup of flour. Stir the batter only enough to combine all the ingredients. Grease baking sheets and put 1½-tablespoon scoops of batter on them. Allow plenty of room for spreading between cookies. Bake in the preheated oven for 13 minutes, or until golden brown around the edges. Cool on racks.

NOTE: You may decorate each scoop of batter with half a hickory nut before baking, like the examples shown on page 43.

SOURCE: *The Lancaster (Pennsylvania) General Hospital "Benefit" Cook Book* (Lancaster, Pa.: Conn & Slote, 1912), 105.

New Years Cakes

1838

New Years Cakes were considered a delicacy most peculiar to New York and the Hudson Valley, but we do find professional bakers in many other East Coast cities advertising these cakes. A baker in Philadelphia advertised in 1840 that he "sells the real New York New Year's Cakes, the genuine Knickerbockers, of all sizes, from a cartwheel to a levenpenny bit."[25]

The eleven-cent piece he referred to was pretty small. It was legal tender in Pennsylvania under the Confederation. Pennsylvanians were not quick to give it up, which is why it was still in circulation in the 1840s.

But how is it that New Years Cakes are also called Knickerbockers? We have already seen this term in connection with the *oliekoecken* in chapter 3. Yes, early Americans were sometimes confused about names, but at least this does tell us is that people in the 1840s were well aware of the Dutch origins of this recipe.

YIELD: APPROXIMATELY 6 DOZEN COOKIES.

6 cups pastry flour
3 cups superfine sugar
1 teaspoon baking powder
½ pound (2 sticks) unsalted butter
1½ teaspoons grated nutmeg
1½ teaspoons caraway seeds
Grated zest of 1 lemon
1 cup milk

Sift the flour, sugar, and baking powder together twice. Put half of the flour mixture into a coarse sieve. Chop the butter into small bits and scatter over the flour. Add the rest of the flour and rub the mixture through the sieve to make a fine crumb. Add the nutmeg, caraway seeds, and lemon zest. Make a hole in the center and add the milk. Work up into a soft dough, cover, and ripen overnight in the refrigerator. The next day, knead the dough until soft and spongy.

Preheat the oven to 325°F.

Roll out the dough, cut into 2-inch rounds, and set on greased baking sheets.

Small New Years Cake print, circa 1835. Marked "E.L.," it once belonged to cookbook writer Eliza Leslie. (Philadelphia Museum of Art)

Bake in the preheated oven 15 to 20 minutes, or until golden brown on the bottom. Cool on racks.

When baking with wooden molds, the baking time will depend on the size of the cookie: the larger the cookie, the longer the baking time. Follow the procedure given in the recipe for Mrs. Crecelius's Springer Cakes on page 149 for preparation of the mold and drying out the cakes overnight before baking.

SOURCE: Eliza Leslie, *Seventy-Five Receipts for Pastry, Cakes, and Sweetmeats* (Boston: Munroe & Francis, 1838), 52–53.

Beware of Camels

CHOCOLATE APEAS

1904

Apeas are a cookie once popular in Philadelphia. The origin of the name is a bit confusing. Essentially, they were a form of *Anis Plätchen* (anise cookies) and stamped *A.P.* to distinguish them from cookies with caraway, which were known as "seed cakes." A great many bakers hawked Apeas to children on the streets. One of those bakers in Philadelphia was Ann Page. The A.P. became associated with her name, if only because her

Anis Plätchen were extremely popular. In any event, A.P. cookies are of German origin. Philadelphians called them Apeas, hence the peculiar name, but to call them anything else—such as Chocolate Apeas, only further muddles the issue. This recipe does not make anise cookies flavored with chocolate; it makes chocolate cookies that taste like Christmas.

YIELD: APPROXIMATELY 5 DOZEN COOKIES.

8 tablespoons (1 stick) unsalted butter
2 cups sugar
½ cup cocoa
1 tablespoon water
¼ teaspoon salt

1 egg
1 teaspoon vanilla extract
2 cups all-purpose flour
1 teaspoon baking soda

Preheat the oven to 350°F.

Cream the butter and sugar, then add the cocoa, water, and salt. Beat the egg and add it and the vanilla extract to the chocolate mixture. Sift the flour and soda together twice, then gradually sift it into the batter.

Roll out the dough between sheets of wax paper ¼ to ½ inch thick. Cut into 2-inch rounds and bake on greased baking sheets in the preheated oven for 15 minutes. Cool on racks.

This dough can be cut into figures like gingerbread or garnished with icing. I scatter vanilla sugar over them as they come from the oven.

SOURCE: Maria Parloa, et al., *Choice Recipes* (Dorchester, Mass.: Walter Baker & Co., 1904), 52.

CHRISTMAS COOKIES

1805

This belongs to a very old family of Hudson Valley recipes known as New York Potash Cake. It is a type of sweet cracker leavened with alkaline salts derived from wood ashes. Today, we use baking soda or baking powder instead. This particular recipe is somewhat like a German Springerle in that it can be stamped with a cookie print. If you wish to stamp these cookies, follow the procedure given under the recipe for Mrs. Creceleius's Springer Cake (page 149).

YIELD: 2½ TO 3 DOZEN COOKIES.

½ cup sugar
¼ cup boiling water
2½ cups pastry flour
½ teaspoon cream of tartar

½ teaspoon baking soda
1½ tablespoons ground coriander
2 tablespoons unsalted butter

Preheat the oven to 350°F.

Dissolve the sugar in the water. Cool, but do not recrystallize. Sift the flour, cream of tartar, baking soda, and coriander together twice. Rub the butter into this and mix thoroughly. Make a hole in the center of the flour and add the cooled syrup. Work this up into a stiff dough and knead it until it becomes elastic and snaps when pulled.

Roll out the dough ¼ inch thick and cut into 2-inch rounds. Bake in the preheated oven on lightly greased baking sheets 15 to 20 minutes, or until pale golden around the edges. Cool on racks.

SOURCE: *New American Cookery* (New York: D. D. Smith, 1805), 66.

Auricula in a pot, a popular Christmas tree ornament in the 1860s and 1870s. Hand colored scrap picture from *The Pictorial Scrap Book* (1860). (Roughwood Collection)

THE LITTLE

New York Cook,

CONTAINING UPWARDS OF

One Thousand Receipts

FOR PREPARING

THE DAILY MEALS

OF

PRIVATE FAMILIES

IN THE MOST

Practical, Wholesome and Frugal Manner.

BY

ANNA MAY.

New York:
PUBLISHED BY E. STEIGER.

Die kleine

New Yorker Köchin,

oder

Anweisung, wie in Familien

die Küche

gut, schmackhaft, abwechselnd

und dabei wohlfeil zu führen ist.

Von

Anna May.

New York:
Verlag von E. Steiger.

A rare German-American cookbook printed in New York in 1859.
(Roughwood Collection.)

HONEY CAKES, OR LEBKUCHEN

1859

This is very close to the Nürnberg Leb-kuchen imported to this country at Christ-mas. The cookies are large, thick, and chewy. Follow my directions explicitly. There is a reason for aging the dough: it undergoes chemical and physical changes essential to the texture and flavor of the cookie.

YIELD: APPROXIMATELY 7 DOZEN COOKIES.

8¾ cups all-purpose flour
2½ tablespoons baking soda
1 tablespoon ground cloves
1 tablespoon ground cinnamon
1 tablespoon ground cardamom
4 cups ground almonds (9 ounces)

½ cup plus 2 tablespoons
chopped citron
2 cups plus 3 tablespoons honey
2 cups plus 3 tablespoons
unsulfured molasses
4 tablespoons brandy

Sift the flour, soda, and spices together twice. Add the ground almonds and citron. Mix the honey and molasses in a saucepan and heat to a gentle boil. Remove from the stove. Make a hole in the center of the flour, and add the honey mixture while still hot. As you stir this into the flour, gradually add the brandy. Work this up into a ball of dough, cover, and set aside to ripen in the refrigerator for 8 days. The dough will rise in bulk as it ripens.

On the eighth day, roll out the dough ¼ inch thick and cut into 2½-inch rounds. Set these on greased baking sheets, cover, and store in a cool place overnight.

Preheat the oven to 325°F.

Bake the cookies 12 to 15 minutes, or until fully risen and pale brown on the bottom. Cool on racks. As they cool, the cookies will harden. Store in airtight containers.

SOURCE: Anna May, *Die kleine New Yorker Köchin* (New York: Verlag von E. Steiger, 1859), 152.

KRINGLES

1846

The name of this cookie refers to the fact that in many parts of Germany, the food gifts left on Christmas Eve were called *Christkindlein,* gifts of the Christ Child. In England, similar food gifts were called Baby Cakes. Both customs trace to the introduction of the Cult of the Bambino Gesú by the Franciscans in the Middle Ages.

In America, *Christkindlein* or *Christkindl* became corrupted in English to Kriss Kringle, who was thought to be the same person as Saint Nicholas. There is a confusing period in the 1840s and 1850s, when we see a great deal about this Kriss Kringle, that is,

until Thomas Nast finally laid him to rest with his creation of the Santa Claus we know today. Nast, incidentally, was born in Landau, Germany, and knew full well the difference between *Christkindlein* and Saint Nicholas.

In any case, Kringles are one of those *Christkindlein* food gifts that German-American children found under (or on) the tree on Christmas morning. Kringles were often made in the form of large, narrow rings.

YIELD: APPROXIMATELY 4 DOZEN 1½-INCH ROUND COOKIES.

---

8 tablespoons (1 stick) unsalted butter
½ cup superfine sugar
6 egg yolks
2 whole eggs

Grated zest of 1 lemon
1 teaspoon lemon extract
3½ cups all-purpose flour

Preheat the oven to 375° F.

Cream the butter and sugar. Beat the eggs to a rich cream and combine with the sugar mixture. Add the lemon zest and extract. Sift the flour into the batter and gradually work it up into a dough. Roll out the dough ¼ inch thick, cut or shape into rings, and set

them on greased baking sheets. Bake in the preheated oven for 10 minutes, or until golden brown on the bottom. Cool on racks.

SOURCE: *Every Lady's Book* (New York: J. K. Wellman, 1846), 45.

CRISP GINGER CAKES

1742

*I*n the original manuscript for Elizabeth El-licott Lea's *Domestic Cookery*—in the possession of one of her descendants—there is considerable marginalia about sources of recipes, dates of testing, and the little alterations she made to recipes based on family practice. In her grandmother's recipe for crisp gingerbread, she calls for ginger, cloves, and coarsely ground anise. The recipe, however, is in all other respects the same as Eliza Smith's, so I have adjusted Smith's to show what some early American cooks could do with English recipes. The anise is definitely an improvement.

YIELD: 8 TO 9 DOZEN 2-INCH COOKIES.

6 cups pastry flour
1½ teaspoons baking powder
1½ tablespoons ground ginger
1 tablespoon ground cloves

1½ tablespoons ground anise
1 cup sugar
1½ cups unsulfured molasses
½ pound (2 sticks) unsalted butter

*S*ift the flour, soda, and spices together in a mixing bowl. Heat the sugar, molasses, and butter in a saucepan over low heat until the butter is melted and the sugar is completely dissolved. Allow to cool a few minutes. Make a hole in the flour and add the molasses mixture. Stir until a very stiff dough forms. Cover and set in the refrigerator to ripen at least 8 hours.

Preheat the oven to 325°F.

Roll out the dough ¼ inch thick and cut into 2-inch rounds. Bake on greased baking sheets in the preheated oven for approximately 15 minutes. Cool on racks.

NOTE: In the seventeenth and early eighteenth centuries, this type of gingerbread was sometimes stamped with decorative patterns and garnished with comfits (sugar-coated caraway or anise seeds).

SOURCE: Eliza Smith, *The Compleat Housewife* (Williamsburg, Va.: Printed and sold by William Parks, 1742), 74.

Crisp Ginger Cakes stamped and ornamented with coriander comfits.

MRS. CRECELIUS'S SPRINGER CAKES

1874

*T*his is a recipe for Springerle cookies, or as the Pennsylvania Dutch call them, *Schpringerkuche*. It comes to us from Mrs. Crecelius, wife of a famous nineteenth-century folk artist and one-time tavern keeper in Bethlehem, Pennsylvania. Her recipe, dated 1874, is preserved in an account book of the Bern Academy, which also doubled as a recipe book for the Epler family of Leesport, Berks County, Pennsylvania.

YIELD: 9 TO 10 DOZEN 2-INCH COOKIES.

5 eggs
2 cups superfine sugar
4½ cups all-purpose flour
1 teaspoon baking soda
1 teaspoon cream of tartar
Grated zest of 1 lemon
Aniseed

*B*eat the eggs to a stiff cream, then fold in the sugar and beat until light. Sift the flour, baking soda, and cream of tartar together twice. Add the lemon zest to the batter, then sift in the flour mixture. Form into a ball and cover. Set in the refrigerator to cool 10 hours.

If you are using a Springerle board, chill it in the refrigerator before using. Brush it very lightly with olive oil, then wipe with a dry cloth. If the mold is particularly elaborate, dust it lightly with flour.

Roll out the dough ½ inch thick when using a cake board. Press the cake board into the dough and gently pull away. Cut out the cookies along the borders (true Springerle cookies have raised borders), and set them on clean baking sheets to dry in a cool, dry place overnight or at least 12 hours. I use an unheated room for this purpose. This step is very important because the drying process keeps the pictures from cracking during baking.

Lacking a board, cut the dough into round cookies.

Preheat the oven to 325°F.

Set the cookies on a lightly greased baking sheet scattered with aniseed and bake 15 to 20 minutes, depending on their size. They are done when the bottoms are golden brown.

SOURCE: Manuscript account book of Bern Academy, Berks County, Pennsylvania, unpaginated. Courtesy of the Library Company of Philadelphia.

Pewter Springerle board by George Endriss of Philadelphia, circa 1880. Each scene depicts a different trade. Can you find the chimney sweep?

SPECULATIUS, Oder Theeletterchen
AN DEN WEIHNACHTSBAUM
1879

The subtitle to this recipe reveals its true character: *Little Tea Cookies for the Christmas Tree*. In other words, it is a good recipe for fancy tin cookie cutters, and the dough is ideal for making tree ornaments because the baked cookies are very lightweight.

YIELD: APPROXIMATELY 9 TO 12 DOZEN COOKIES.

3½ cups all-purpose flour
1 teaspoon baking powder
½ pound (2 sticks) unsalted butter
2 cups superfine sugar

8 tablespoons ground cinnamon
Grated zest of 1 lemon
3 eggs

Sift the flour and baking powder together twice. Then rub the butter, sugar, and flour mixture to a fine crumb using a sieve. Add the cinnamon and lemon zest. Beat the eggs to a froth. Make a hole in the center of the crumbs and add the eggs. Stir and work this up into a dough. Cover and ripen overnight in the refrigerator.

Preheat the oven to 350° F.

Roll out the dough ¼ inch thick—this thickness is critical. Cut with a fancy tin cutter or, lacking that, with a sharp knife. Set the cookies on greased baking sheets.

Bake in the preheated oven approximately 13 minutes. Cool on racks.

NOTE: If you cut out holes in the center of each cookie, the cookies will be even crisper and more delicate. Furthermore, with a little hole in each one, you will have something to loop the ribbon through when you hang the cookies on the Christmas tree.

SOURCE: Henrietta Davidis, *Praktisches Kochbuch für die Deutschen in Amerika* (Milwaukee, Wis.: W. Georg Brumlers Verlag, 1879), 278.

Pretzel mold for speculatius. (Courtesy of the Deutsches Brotmuseum, Ulm, Germany)

SUGAR JUMBLES

—— 1825 ——

YIELD: APPROXIMATELY 4 DOZEN COOKIES.

½ pound (2 sticks) unsalted butter
1½ cups superfine sugar
2 eggs

2 teaspoons caraway seeds
3½ cups pastry flour
Confectioners' sugar

Cream the butter and sugar until fluffy. Beat the eggs to a froth and combine with the sugar mixture. Add the caraway seeds. Sift in the flour gradually and work it up into a soft dough. Cover and ripen in the refrigerator 24 hours.

Preheat oven to 325°F.

Roll the dough into a long rope, ½ inch thick. Cut this into 4-inch segments and join them into rings. Smooth and shape with the fingers, then dip each ring in confectioners' sugar. Set on greased baking sheets and bake in the preheated oven 20 to 25 minutes, or until golden brown on the bottom. Cool on racks.

NOTE: The surface of the jumbles will cool with a frosted appearance. They should be very crisp. In earlier times they were favored for dunking in hot tea, coffee, or cider.

SOURCE: Eliza Dodge Romeyn, manuscript recipe and poetry book, Columbia County, New York, 1825, unpaginated. Roughwood Collection.

Tin jumble or doughnut cutter, circa 1875–1885.

WAFER JUMBLES
1867

Another name for Wafer Jumbles was Paper Jumbles, which should give you some idea how *thin* they ought to be. This recipe comes from the manuscript cookbook of Carrie Ayres Lockwood of Norwalk, Connecticut.

YIELD: APPROXIMATELY 8 DOZEN COOKIES.

1 pound (4 sticks) unsalted butter
2 cups superfine sugar
4 eggs
Grated zest of 1 lemon

1 teaspoon lemon extract
4¼ cups all-purpose flour
Confectioners' sugar (see note)

Cream the butter and sugar. Beat the eggs to a froth and combine with the sugar mixture. Add the lemon zest and extract. Gradually sift in the flour and work this into a soft dough. Cover and ripen in the refrigerator 2 to 3 hours. The dough must be kept very cold or it will become difficult to work with.

Preheat the oven to 325°F.

Liberally dust the work surface, rolling pin and hands with confectioners' sugar. Break off a piece of cold dough and roll as thin as possible. Cut out cookies with a doughnut cutter and lay them on ungreased baking sheets. Bake in the preheated oven for approximately 12 minutes. Remove from the baking sheets as quickly as possible and cool on racks. Store away from the humidity in airtight containers.

NOTE: Wafer jumbles should be very crisp and slightly golden around the outside edge. Baking parchment sometimes helps alleviate sticking, but it all depends on the type of metal in your baking sheet.

For the above proportions, roughly two-thirds of a 1-pound box of confectioners' sugar will be needed in making the cookies. If the dough seems too soft due to weather conditions, work just enough confectioners' sugar into it to make it easy to handle. Wiping the surface of each jumble with confectioners' sugar before it is baked will create a bubbly crisp texture on the top of the cookies.

SOURCE: Carrie Ayres Lockwood, manuscript cookbook, Norwalk, Connecticut, 1867, unpaginated. Quoted with the kind permission of the Lockwood-Mathews Mansion, Norwalk, Connecticut.

The house where Carrie Ayres Lockwood made her wafer jumbles.
From a nineteenth-century engraving. (Courtesy of the
Lockwood-Mathews Mansion, Norwalk, Connecticut)

SIX

Who Said *Plum* Pudding?

"P is for Plum Pudding, a rich one I own."[1] Lines like this, repeated over and over in Victorian children's books, drove home the popular notion that plum pudding was indeed the "Crown of the Christmas Table," the very measure of Christmas itself.[2]

The trophy on the following page, dense as a cannonball but many times larger, certainly fulfills all of the Victorian era fantasies about marvelous size and Yuletide grandeur. Yet let's be realistic: I rather doubt our Christmas cook could lift it. I suspect she had some trouble boiling it, considering that a small one required about six hours of steady cooking. And I am certain that dyspepsia followed, although it was slow to dampen the old-time passion for anything made with "plums."

This brings us to a family of related dishes, all of which were originally made of meat and had very little to do with plums as we now know them. Over the centuries, as these dishes gradually became sweeter with the addition of dried fruits (and eventually sugar), the proportion of meat declined, as in mincemeat pie, or it disappeared altogether, as in plum porridge or plum pudding.

In the case of the Little Plumcakes in the previous chapter, the "plums" were zante currants. In the case of Twelfth Night Cake, the "plums" were a mixture of currants and raisins. In both of these recipes, the word

American Plum Pudding baked in a yellowware dish, two Suet Puddings in Boston cups, and Steamed Fruit Pudding as prepared in a tin pudding bucket.

Plum pudding advertisement from 1911. (Roughwood Collection)

plum meant dried fruit, any dried fruit, any extra ingredient that enhanced a recipe by making it rich and more expensive, or simply better in the eyes of a particular cook. Used in this sense, "plums" could be anything from dried dates and figs to dried cherries, dried blueberries, or even dried apples and peaches. The easiest way to keep it all straight is to remember that in English cookery—and early American cookery— "plums" were any sort of dried fruit that resembled prunes in color or sweetness.

Out of this evolved a related term *sugarplum,* the sweetmeats (candied fruit) that went into rich cakes and puddings. More specifically, in the lingo of professional confectioners in the eighteenth and nineteenth centuries, sugarplums were comfits (candied coriander or caraway seeds or aniseeds). In the seventeenth century, comfits were often added to cakes, which may partially explain the reason for this particular use of the term.

During the Middle Ages, the first domesticated plums used in English cookery were the dried plums sent over from France and the Mediterranean countries. At that time, plums were considered a great luxury, the best part of the dish, certainly worthy of the elaborate recipes connected with Christmas feasting. And rather like gilding the lily, expensive, imported dried fruits were added to meat dishes to make them more impressive and appealing to medieval taste.

After England entered into special trade agreements with Portugal in the 1300s (there was a royal marriage involved), Por-tuguese raisins seem to have pushed other types of dried fruit out of English Christmas recipes. In the 1600s, with the introduction of zante currants into English cookery, the term "plum" was extended to include currants as well. It is not surprising that in English folk cookery, where economics forced country cooks to use cheap local ingredients rather than imported fare, plum pudding was often made with dried haws, sloes, and other types of wild fruit in the plum family. On this point, the old folk recipes may approximate medieval forms of the dish.

In the 1850s, Mrs. Horace Mann took potshots at plum pudding in her *Christianity in the Kitchen.* While she listed a plum pudding in her index, the recipe she provided was actually boiled bread pudding held together with eggs.[3] Not a bad substitute considering her excessive entanglements with fig lemonades, toast waters, and cauliflower purées. Mrs. Mann was a food faddist, a rather influential one in her day. Yet it was not the "plums" in plum pudding that so provoked her; it was the waxen suet and the difficult digestibility of such dense, heavy cookery.

Beyond this, there is an unspoken objection in her writing to almost anything connected with butchering, and this brings us full circle to that loose but meaty connection between plum porridges, plum puddings, and mincemeats. Because of our highly urbanized life-style today, we are largely disconnected from the old calendrical cycles associated with farming and feasting. But it is in this

Who Said Plum Pudding?

From a children's ABC book, circa 1840. (Roughwood Collection)

old agricultural context that we must look to understand why plum pudding and its related dishes were so significant in Christmas cookery. In essence, plum puddings, plum porridges, and mincemeat pies were all variations of the same root concept: they were types of glorified sausage. Sausage making was planned around Advent.

Advent is the traditional beginning of the Christmas season. According to the Christian church calendar, it is a three-week period starting on the first Sunday after November 26. Before the Reformation, this was a period of fasting, as it remains for many Catholics even today. For this reason butchering normally took place prior to November 26 or more commonly immediately following the last Sunday in Advent in order to guarantee meat and puddings for Christmas. It was perhaps no coincidence that the Puritan Thanksgiving of New England, which served as a substitute for Christmas,

was fixed in this old period for slaughtering. In short, it did not conflict with the folk calendar and popular custom.

Butchering shortly before Christmas was also practical. Cold weather helped preserve the meat and the timing ensured that the meat would be consumed before it spoiled. Most Protestant churches did away with the old period of fasting with the result that Christmas cooks were often faced with logistical difficulties of the sort related in a letter from Mrs. William H. Cook of Ticonderoga, New York, to her daughter-in-law, dated December 7, 1883: "We killed our hog, and cow on Monday, and have made sausages, head cheese, fried lard, and tallow, and today I feel as if I had got through butchering, for I am all done except boiling my meat for mince pies. We wish you were here to help us eat up some of our goodies for the weather is so warm that we are afraid it will spoil."[4]

The Christmas dish most familiar to us in Mrs. Cook's letter is mincemeat pie, also called *Christmas Pie* both here and in England.[5] It is peculiarly Anglo-American in so far as it is a survivor from the Middle Ages that died out in the cookery of Continental Europe by the seventeenth century. Europeans now find it odd that we mix sugar with meat.

Minced or pounded meats, indeed any food ground up to a fine consistency, was once considered elegant, refined, a measure of high status not just because of the pleasing texture but also because of the extraordinary

The Christmas Cook

Still life with Mincemeat Pie, attributed to Pieter Claesz,
circa 1630. (Art Institute of Chicago)

amount of work that went into creating it. We find this texture in many dishes of medieval origin: *haggis* of Scotland, mincemeat pies, and the old French pâtés baked in crusts, just to name a few. All of these types of dishes were referred to as *hashmeats* in English, a word that survives today in such varied recipe names as corned beef hash, hashed chicken, and hash browns (chopped fried potatoes). In practice, we eat hashmeat every time we eat sausage, be it liverwurst or bologna, or any species of lunch meat made by grinding and pressing the ingredients; even hamburger is a hashmeat. Mix sugar, wine, chopped apples, and raisins with hamburger and we step back in time to a typical mincemeat filling for pie. The great standing pies with ornamental crusts in which mincemeat was usually baked were one practical method for cooking this dish and getting it to the table.

Quite often, the standing crusts were inedible, made as they were from rye flour and hot water. They served as throwaway containers that were given to beggars or distributed to the poor, or simply thrown to the pigs. Rich standing crusts, such as Charlotte Mason's on page 99, were generally reserved for the smaller sorts of pies like the one for which I have provided a recipe.

It comes from *The Compleat Cook* of 1658 and shows up repeatedly in American recipe collections of the eighteenth and nineteenth centuries, a certain testimonial to its immense popularity. We find it, for example, in the 1815 recipe of Rosina Hubley published

Pastry cutter designs for crust ornaments on mincemeat pies. From Joseph Cooper's *The Art of Cookery* (1654). (Roughwood Collection)

many years later in a charitable cookbook from Lancaster, Pennsylvania.[6] Large standing mincemeat pies were quite popular in the Middle Colonies. But as they cut such a magnificent impression at the table, Puritans railed against them as worship of luxury, or as one critic put it: "Idolatrie in crust!"[7]

Let it be said that the New Englanders had their own forms of "idolatrie," for it was common practice in that part of the country to set fire to roast turkeys by dousing them with brandy before delivering them to the table.[8] This was thought to improve the flavor of the skin.

In the Middle Colonies, this practice was similarly applied to mincemeat pies, in part to caramelize the sugar scattered on the crust. The ever-observant Miss Eliza Leslie considered this old-fashioned custom coarse in the extreme. In her *New Cookery Book* of 1857, she remarked rather acidly: "The foolish custom of setting the pies on fire after they come to the table and causing a blue blaze to issue from the liquor that is in them,

The Christmas Cook

is now obsolete, and considered ungenteel and tavern-like. If this practice originated in a polite desire to *frighten the ladies,* its purpose is already a failure, for the ladies are not frightened; that is, not really."[9]

A neater, more humble way of serving mincemeat was to use it as filling inside pockets of crust called Pasties or Fried Pies —like the recipe described in chapter 1. In America, pasties eventually fell out of fashion in favor of lighter snack foods; today they survive only in the upper Midwest. Yet they were once as popular as they still are in England. And in the Eastern states, where they were often baked in six-inch earthenware saucers, they were known by yet another name: *saucer pies.*[10]

Saucer pies were eaten as portable snacks in much the same manner that we carry about sandwiches today, or as a breakfast or supper dish, in which case they took the place of fresh sausage. It was not unusual for a family to put up as much mincemeat for the winter as sausage. Both were stored in large crocks, but mincemeat kept better because alcohol was added in the form of wine, brandy, or applejack—one reason for those vulgar blue flames Miss Leslie objected to.

Another species of hashmeat was plum porridge or plum pottage, which might well be styled a mincemeat pie served as stew. I have provided a recipe for it from Richard Brigg's *New Art of Cookery,* published in Philadelphia in 1792, more as a study piece than a recipe to be used. On the other hand, let it be a challenge to your palate!

I am certain that this festal pottage was one of the customs referred to in the December 1821 *Literary Journal,* which noted: "Christmas is still kept as a festival in some parts of America, together with many old English usages which are no more seen in the mother country."[11] The variations are infinite and the dish meets the needs of the poorer Christmas cooks who could not af-

Saucer Pie (TOP) baked in an earthenware pie dish and a group of small tin pie saucers. On the left, Hickory Nut Macaroons (PAGE 236).

Who Said Plum Pudding?

ford lavish ingredients or who did not have the proper equipment to make grand pies or fancy bag puddings. Cheap cuts of meat (shins for example) boiled to shreds would serve as well as any. In fact, meat was often dispensed with altogether.

English food historian Elizabeth David believes that plum porridge predates plum pudding. I am convinced that she is correct in this assessment, since boiled "bag" puddings like plum pudding did not enter general English cookery until the seventeenth century. Furthermore, one can easily visualize the medieval antecedents of plum porridge in a pottage called *mawmeny* (shredded pheasant meat, quince paste, ginger, spices, etc.) and in glorified forms of *frumenty*.[12] Early American recipes for frumenty, a porridge made with whole grains, usually wheat, are common—even the Puritans made frumenty. So too are the dishes made from the starchy liquid cooked out of whole or pounded grains. This congeals into a pudding called flummery, long considered a health food by our ancestors.

Victorians had a love-hate relationship with Christmas plum pudding. Doctors said it was unfit to eat, yet at holiday time, caution went to the winds. This probably had much to do with the image that the pudding projected, what it represented as opposed to what was inside. Plum pudding was a symbol of hospitality, of a Christmas centering not around the tree, but on the family sitting around the table. It was free of the theological tensions inherent in other aspects of Christmas feasting, and it was highly nostalgic. Perhaps it is not coincidental that these massive boiled puddings declined in popularity in this country with the concurrent rise in popularity of the Christmas tree. With the spread of the tree to all parts of the United States complete by 1900, the secular focus had shifted from pudding to greenery.

This decline did not go unnoticed or unlamented. We see obvious attempts to sustain the pudding tradition with inoculations of Christian virtue, as in Mary J. Barr's 1903 article for the *Cooking Club Magazine:* "The Christmas pudding is supposed to be emblematical of the rich offerings made by the three kings to the infant in the stable at Bethlehem."[13] Suet for the Baby? This kind of mythology came too late to do much good, not to mention that it shifted attention to Twelfth Night, where it came in conflict with other customs.

Furthermore, even by the early nineteenth century, Americans generally viewed the Great Plum Pudding as something urban and upper class and more particularly English than typical of our general Christmas fare. By this time, we had developed a host of other plum puddings far more edible and far less formidable, and better suited to the informality of our national character. Among these I would place American Plum Pudding first because it is one of the oldest.

American Plum Pudding is a species of custard. It is made with milk baked at a low temperature over a long period of time until it coagulates into a junketlike consistency.

The Christmas Cook

This type of pudding and the technique for making it appeared in New England in the seventeenth century. It is often called Yankee Plum Pudding in acknowledgment of this origin.

Other types of plum pudding would include Mary Barr's pudding steam baked in a tin—the same technique as Victorian Boston Brown Bread—which I have provided on page 177; the 1887 fruit pudding done in a vegetable steamer, a clever American innovation; and the Suet Pudding baked in Boston cups. Boston cups were yellowware or stoneware custard cups once extremely popular in New England, but also widely sold in other parts of the country.

The steam-baked pudding can be done in a variety of molds, the most common being the so-called bucket with a center tube, followed very closely by the melon mold. The melon mold permitted the Christmas cook to make a plum pudding that at least came out with a roundish shape, although nothing quite as spectacular as the old-style orbs boiled in pudding bags. I should add that very few pudding bags made puddings as perfectly globelike as the ones shown in pictures. The sheer weight of the puddings made them sag (or split open!) when turned out onto the serving dish. In any case, at right I have illustrated a pudding bag since it has now become an endangered species. The bag was made for me by Alice Schankweiler Parkyn of Shamokin, Pennsylvania. A lady now in her eighties, Alice was trained as a child to make pudding bags for her mother,

The pudding bag has been filled with a plum pudding, tied down with the drawstring, and then tied to the handle of the kettle in which it will be boiled.

who operated a baking and pastry business.

Pudding bags look like small pillowcases with long drawstrings at the open end. The drawstring allowed the cook to pull the bag tight and then to tie it around the middle or at whatever level she chose, depending on

Who Said Plum Pudding?

the size of the pudding. The remainder of the string was then tied to the handle of the pot in which the pudding was to be boiled so the whole thing could be fished out when it was done without scalding the fingers.

Pudding bags were usually made of coarse linen or reused cotton flour sacks; size depended on personal taste, but preferences seem to have run in favor of the 5-pound bags. All the bags made for me by Alice Parkyn were made from flour bags dating from about 1910–1915. They were first washed to remove any pictures or printing on them, then they were bleached.

Not everyone found steamed or boiled puddings agreeable to their digestive systems. One popular substitute was plum pudding ice cream, which was made in a variety

of ways, sometimes flavored with chocolate, sometimes filled with nuts, other times brightly colored, as in the case of Kentucky Cream (page 168), which is supposed to be pink.

It was the professional confectioners like James Parkinson of Philadelphia, Ferra's of Boston, Charles Gunther of Chicago, and John Meyer of Cincinnati who led the way during the nineteenth century in putting up Christmas puddings and ices in fancy molds. Under the headline "Preparing for the Holidays," the Alhambra Confectionery in Philadelphia, for example, advertised in 1848 not only molded water ices, ice creams, and jellies (sweet gelatins), but various fancy Christmas cakes as well, all delivered to the door for a small extra charge.[14] Christmas

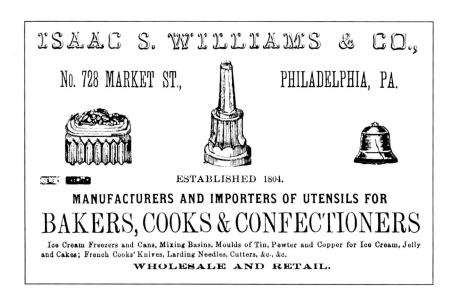

From *The Confectioners' Journal*, March 1876.

cooks, particularly in large towns, were always able to augment their menus with store-bought dishes.

For the truly dyspeptic, there were of course a variety of other foods prepared for the holidays. Flummeries were always recommended, and rice dishes in particular were given high priority. Among these we find Saint Nicholas pudding, a curious mixture of fakelore and health fetish.

Saint Nicholas Pudding is straightforward rice flummery garnished with meringue. It appears in a variety of old cookbooks under many other guises: Queen of Puddings, Queen's Pudding, and Iced Rice Pudding, to name a few. A similar pudding made with cornstarch rather than rice was called Delmonico Pudding, after the famous restaurant in New York. Saint Nicholas pudding, however, was made almost exclusively for children, and I suspect that the enticing name was partly an inducement to get them to eat it while the adults nibbled on something more substantial and alcoholic. The association with Saint Nicholas is also an attempt to create a sense of connectedness with a Dutch colonial heritage, taking into account that the recipe came from the Dutch Reformed Church in Passaic, New Jersey.

A colonial connection is much more obvious in pumpkin pudding, which we now call pumpkin pie. Like the recipe for potato pudding, it was traditionally baked in a large shallow, saucerlike dish, a more spacious version of the dishes used for making saucer

On the left, a china melon mold for flummery and other starch-based puddings. On the right, tin pudding molds from the 1876 advertisement on the opposite page.

pies. The plates were lined with short pastry in part to protect the delicate pudding from burning as it baked. The crust rim was often highly decorated. Some cooks had carved pastry wheels for impressing decorative devices into the dough.

In the North, pumpkin pudding is associated with Thanksgiving and Christmas. In the Chesapeake Bay area, white potato pudding is still served at Christmas and New Years. Farther South, white potato pudding is replaced with sweet potato pudding, a dish that today has developed a firm association with the Afro-American New Years. It was one of the dishes originally baked for Jubilee.

Who Said Plum Pudding?

POTATO PUDDING

1894

*T*his is an old Christmas and New Years pudding that is still popular on the eastern shore of Maryland, where it is often called Pudding Pie. It is advisable to treat this as a soufflé, since it is best as it comes from the oven.

YIELD: 8 TO 10 SERVINGS.

1 pound white potatoes (weight after paring)
½ pound (2 sticks) unsalted butter
8 egg yolks
1 teaspoon ground mace
Grated zest and juice of 1 lemon
2 cups sugar
½ cup chopped citron
4 egg whites

*P*eel and weigh the potatoes. Boil until soft, drain, and while still hot, beat in the butter to form a batter. Let this cool until lukewarm, then beat the egg yolks to a froth and combine with the potatoes. Add the mace and lemon zest and juice. Beat again; add the sugar and beat until light. Fold in the citron. Beat the egg whites until stiff and fold them in as well.

Pour the batter into a well-greased baking dish measuring approximately 2 by 9 by 12 inches and bake 35 to 40 minutes, or until set in the middle. Serve immediately.

SOURCE: Mrs. Charles H. Gibson. *Maryland and Virginia Cook Book* (Baltimore: John Murphy & Co., 1894), 152–53.

Chromolithograph trade card, circa 1876. (Roughwood Collection)

AMERICAN PLUM PUDDING

1839

This is what many early Americans meant when they said plum pudding. It is served hot or cold in soup bowls with cream and sugar, sweetened stewed fruit, or whole pre- served strawberries. I highly recommend the latter.

YIELD: 8 TO 10 SERVINGS.

½ cup fine cracker crumbs
7 cups milk
8 eggs
¾ cup lemon juice

1 tablespoon grated nutmeg
2 cups raisins
1 tablespoon flour

Mix the cracker crumbs and 1 cup of milk. Let this stand for 2 to 3 hours.

Preheat the oven to 300°F.

Add the remaining milk to the crumbs and beat vigorously to make a thin batter. Beat the eggs to a froth and combine with the milk mixture. Add the lemon juice and nut- meg. Dust the raisins with 1 tablespoon of flour. Either fold them into the batter or scat- ter them evenly over the bottom of two well- greased baking dishes measuring roughly 9 by 12 by 2 inches. Add the batter, distribut- ing it evenly in both dishes. Set the puddings on the lowest rack in your oven and bake for 1 hour 35 minutes or until the centers have set. Serve hot or cold.

SOURCE: *The Approved Recipe Book* (Plainfield, N.J.: M. F. Cushing, 1839), 15.

KENTUCKY CREAM

1885

*T*his frozen dessert is the recipe of Mrs. J. B. McCreary, wife of the governor of Kentucky in the 1880s. I have added rum, which greatly enhances the flavor.

YIELD: 15 TO 20 SERVINGS.

1½ cups currants
2 tablespoons blanched slivered almonds
½ cup chopped citron
¾ cup golden rum
4¼ cups milk

¾ cup sugar
4 whole eggs
4 egg yolks
1 envelope unflavored gelatin
2 cups strawberry preserves
2 cups heavy cream

*P*ut the currants, almonds, and citron in a bowl and add ¼ of the cup of rum. Cover and let stand overnight. The next day scald 4 cups of milk and dissolve the sugar in it. Beat the eggs until light, then pour them into a double boiler over low heat. Gradually add the scalded milk, whisking as you pour to keep it from curdling the eggs. While the custard is heating in the double boiler, dissolve the gelatin in the remaining milk. Bring the custard to a gentle boil, stirring constantly until it thickens. Add the gelatin, whisk smooth, and remove from the heat.

Pour mixture into a pan, cover, and set in a deep freezer. As soon as the custard begins to freeze, drain and add the currants, almonds, and citron, and the strawberry preserves. Reserve the rum. Whisk the heavy cream until stiff and fold it into the custard. Add the reserved rum to the remaining

½ cup of rum, stir well, and pour the mixture into a clean mold. Freeze 2 days.

To unmold the ice cream, dip a towel in cold water and wring it out. Wrap the towel around the mold, remove the lid, and turn the mold up. The ice cream should slide out within a few seconds. If it does not, dip the towel in cold water again, wring it out and repeat. Do not run hot water over the mold. This will cause the ice cream to melt and when it finally comes out, it will have lost its ornamental shape.

NOTE: It is wise to put a paper doilie or a napkin on the serving dish you plan to use for the ice cream. This will help prevent the ice cream from sliding off as you carry it to the dining room.

SOURCE: Mrs. E. R. Tennent, *House-Keeping in the Sunny South* (Atlanta: Jas. P. Harrison Co., 1885), 198.

Plombiere mold of tinned copper for frozen desserts, circa 1885.

Who Said Plum Pudding?

SUET PUDDING

1903

The benefit of this recipe is that it can be made in individual helpings small enough to satisfy even the most guilt-ridden weight watchers.

YIELD: 8 TO 12 SERVINGS.

2½ cups all-purpose flour
2 teaspoons ground ginger
1 cup chopped suet (page 179)
1 cup chopped raisins
½ cup currants
1 cup milk
1 cup unsulfured molasses

Preheat the oven to 325°F.

Combine all the ingredients in a large work bowl. Grease the interiors of small custard cups and fill the cups to within ½ inch of the rim. Set the cups in pans of hot water to a depth of no less than halfway up each cup in the preheated oven. Bake for 1½ hours or until done in the center. Replenish the water in the pans if it should cook off too rapidly.

SOURCE: Mary J. Barr, "The Christmas Pudding," *Cooking Club Magazine* 5 (December 1903), 554.

LARGEST ASSORTMENT

—OF—

SCRAP ✕ PICTURES,

—AND THE—

CHEAPEST PLACE TO BUY

—IS AT—

JOHN H. RITTER'S NEW BOOKSTORE,

9 SOUTH EIGHTH ST., ALLENTOWN, PA.

PUMPKIN PUDDING

1849

This dish has a definite relationship to the American Plum Pudding on page 167 in that it is a custardy dessert slow baked at a low temperature. Pumpkin purée is used in place of the cracker crumbs.

Opinion differed, however, on many points of serving. One New England housewife claimed: "Pumpkin pie is better a few days old, or when the top begins to look shiny." [15] To this, another housewife responded: "We presume the lady who keeps her pumpkin pies till they shine on top, prefers them in just that state of ripeness; but in our estimation this is but half a hair's breadth from souring, and if by any oversight a pie had reached that precarious condition, we should call in our neighbors to help dispose of it forthwith, for we would rather have our food when it is new and fresh—especially in warm weather—and think the above mentioned pies are never better than at breakfast the morning after they are baked." [16] Pies for breakfast—this may help explain why the cook with the barrel of flour in chapter 4 baked 94 pies in one month.

YIELD: 8 SERVINGS.

1 quart milk	2 teaspoons salt
3 eggs	Grated zest of 1 lemon
2 cups pumpkin purée	2 tablespoons ground cinnamon
1 cup unsulfured molasses	1 tablespoon ground ginger

Preheat the oven to 300°F.

Butter a shallow baking dish with a 2-quart capacity. Beat the milk and eggs together, then combine with the pumpkin purée. Add the molasses, salt, lemon, and spices. Pour this into the baking dish and set the dish in a pan of boiling water (see note). Place in the preheated oven and bake 1 hour 35 to 40 minutes, or until set in the center.

If you prefer to bake this in pie shells, preheat the oven to 425°F. Line four 9-inch pie plates with My Paste Royal (page 95), but double the quantities given for the crust. Fill the pies with the pumpkin mixture and bake in the preheated oven for 10 minutes. Reduce heat to 350°F, and continue baking for 40 minutes.

NOTE: The water need only come up 1 or 2 inches on the side of the baking dish. Its purpose here is twofold: to protect the bottom of the pudding from scorching and to keep the humidity in the oven as high as possible.

SOURCE: James M. Sanderson, *The Complete Cook* (Philadelphia: Larry & Getz, 1849), 160–61.

SNOW BALLS

1787

*T*his recipe appears in old cookbooks sometimes under cakes, sometimes under dumplings. It is a festive little dish that looks very handsome on old Canton china.

YIELD: 5 SERVINGS.

5 tart cooking apples
5 tablespoons quince or
orange marmalade

1 batch My Paste Royal (page 95)
Royal Icing (page 127)

*P*reheat the oven to 350°F.

Pare and core the apples, but do not remove the blossom ends. Shave the bottoms so that the apples stand level. Put 1 tablespoon of marmalade in each apple. Roll out the pie pastry and wrap each apple in dough. Gently roll the apples in your hands to press the dough tight and to smooth out any seams. Prick the apples on top and set them in a greased baking dish. Bake in the preheated oven 25 to 35 minutes or until the apples are slightly underbaked. Overbaking will cause the apples to sag and the dough to split open.

Remove the apples from the oven and cool on racks. When cool, drip Royal Icing over them until a thick layer forms. Let the icing harden, then, to quote John Farley, "Put one in the middle of a dish, and the others round it." And so serve them forth.

NOTE: My experience has been that 5 apples rarely come through this experiment holding their shape. You might consider wrapping the dough-covered apples with cheesecloth, then baking them. Remove the cloth once the apples are cool. This will help them keep their round shape and give you a rough surface that will take the icing better. The icing may be flavored with cinnamon oil, rosewater, or lemon juice.

SOURCE: John Farley, *The London Art of Cookery* (London: Printed for J. Scatcherd and J. Whitaker, 1787), 327.

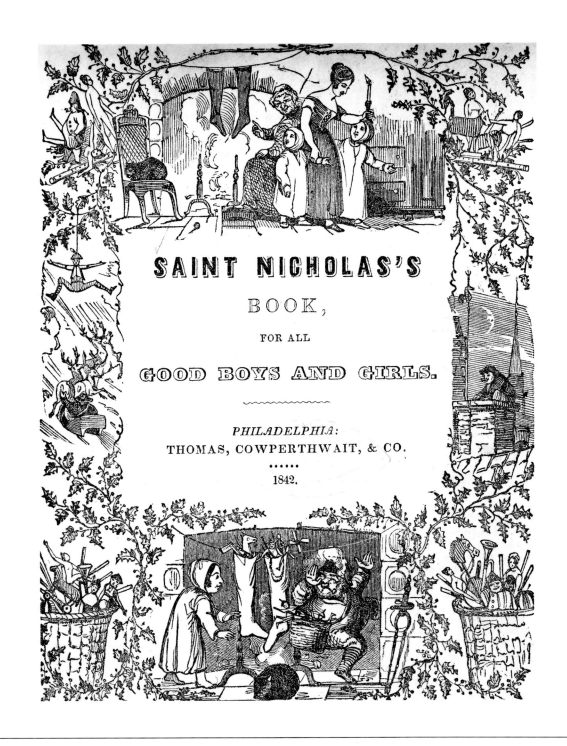

SAINT NICHOLAS'S

BOOK,

FOR ALL

GOOD BOYS AND GIRLS.

PHILADELPHIA:
THOMAS, COWPERTHWAIT, & CO.

......

1842.

SAINT NICHOLAS PUDDING

YIELD: 8 TO 10 SERVINGS.

¾ cup pounded rice (see note)
¼ teaspoon salt
1 quart milk
½ cup sugar
3 eggs, separated

1½ tablespoons vanilla extract
4 to 6 drops essence of bitter almond,
or to taste
2 tablespoons superfine sugar

Simmer the rice in salted milk until soft (30 to 35 minutes). Whisk from time to time to beat out lumps. Once the rice is cooked, add the sugar. Preheat the oven to 350°F.

Beat the egg yolks and gradually whisk them into the pudding. Continue whisking until the mixture thickens (about 5 minutes). Add the vanilla and almond flavorings. Pour the batter into a greased 2-quart soufflé dish. Beat the egg whites until stiff, then beat in the superfine sugar. Spread this over the pudding and brown in the oven for 10 minutes. Serve hot or cold.

NOTE: Broken rice is available in some parts of the South, but it is not as fine as old-style pounded rice, which was prepared by beating whole, hulled rice in a mortar. The result was similar to corn grits, but unlike grits, the more pounded rice was whisked as it cooked, the smoother and creamier it became.

It is possible to make the equivalent of old-style pounded rice by putting the rice in a food processor and running the cutting blade in pulses. Sift out the largest pieces and pound them in a mortar. Use everything, even the fine rice flour that gathers in the bottom of the mortar. Both broken rice and pounded rice are more flavorful than whole rice.

Rice flour is also an alternative; its use results in a thicker pudding.

SOURCE: North Reformed Church, *Cooks in Clover* (Passaic, N.J.: Thurston & Barker, 1889), 65.

PLUM PORRIDGE FOR CHRISTMAS

1792

I have cut this recipe to one-eighth of the original, and it still makes enough for a respectable dinner. Naturally, a large-batch recipe such as this implies that it was intended in the eighteenth century for a mammoth Christmas feast, enough for everyone on the plantation and perhaps the neighborhood as well. For all its elaborate ingredients, the porridge lacks one thing: fat. I can honestly say that aside from being pleasantly unusual, it is also low in cholesterol. I have sweetened it according to period taste, but if you want, you can reduce the sugar.

YIELD: APPROXIMATELY 8 SERVINGS.

3 pounds beef bones for stewing
1 gallon water
1¾ cups white bread crumbs
2¼ cups currants
1½ cups raisins
¾ cup chopped pitted prunes

1 cup brown sugar
1½ teaspoons ground mace
1½ teaspoons ground cloves
1½ teaspoons grated nutmeg
1 cup white wine or sherry
Lemon juice

*B*oil the beef bones in the water for 2 hours, skimming the scum as it rises. Strain the broth and reserve 3 cups. Clean the pot and put the remaining broth in it. Use the meat from the bones for another dish, such as mincemeat pie.

Pour the 3 cups of reserved broth over the bread crumbs and let them stand for 45 minutes. While the bread crumbs are soaking, add the currants, raisins, prunes, sugar, spices, and wine to the broth you have returned to the pot. Simmer for 45 minutes.

Purée the soaked bread crumbs to a batter consistency in a blender or food processor. Gradually add this to the stew, whisking as you add it to keep it from forming lumps.

Simmer 20 minutes and serve in porringers. Squeeze a little lemon juice over the top of each serving. The porridge may be frozen for later use.

NOTE: Since the seventeenth century, it appears that the meat was held out of most of the plum porridge recipes. But originally it was added. Some recipes used oatmeal or barley instead of white bread. Several recipes mention storing the porridge in earthenware pans. In America, this was usually done in the springhouse or dairy, or if the weather was cool enough, in the attic.

SOURCE: Richard Briggs, *The New Art of Cookery* (Philadelphia: W. Spotswood, R. Campbell, and B. Johnson, 1792), 52.

PLUM PUDDING

1903

YIELD: APPROXIMATELY 8 TO 10 SERVINGS.

3 cups bread crumbs
2 cups raisins
2 cups currants
1 cup chopped citron
1 cup brown sugar
½ cup diced salt pork
8 tablespoons (1 stick) unsalted
butter, chopped

¼ teaspoon ground cloves
½ teaspoon ground mace
1 teaspoon ground allspice
1 teaspoon ground cinnamon
1 egg
Milk

Preheat the oven to 350°F. Brown the bread crumbs in the preheated oven for 8 to 10 minutes, or until golden. Remove from the oven and cool.

Mix all of the ingredients in a large work bowl and moisten with only enough milk to give it the consistency of croquettes. Grease the interior of a tin pudding mold and dust it with flour. Shake out any excess flour. Gently pack the pudding mixture into the mold. Fasten the lid tightly (it should have clamps) so that no steam can escape. Set the mold in a large pot of boiling water. The water should reach the rim of the mold, or the pudding will cook in two parts. Boil 6 to 8 hours gently and continuously, or until the pudding is done. Turn out of the mold and serve hot with butter or wine sauce.

SOURCE: Mary J. Barr, "The Christmas Pudding," *Cooking Club Magazine* 5 (December 1903), 554.

Who Said Plum Pudding?

MINCEMEAT PIE

1658

The original recipe called upon us to use 3½ pounds of suet, *far more* than enough! That was the age in English cookery when meat pies after baking were filled to overflowing with melted butter. My impression of those hardy people is that they had skin like tallow and blood vessels like rope.

I had a rather long and interesting discussion once with Ann Willan (president of Ecole de Cuisine La Varenne) about the properties of suet. She, being from Yorkshire, spoke with rare authority. I had to admit, after some initial squeamishness, that she was absolutely right: the culinary effects peculiar to suet cannot be reproduced in other ways. In mincemeat and plum pudding, this is especially so, for there is a texture and flavor that is incomparable—when done right.

YIELD: ENOUGH FOR TWO 9-INCH PIES, 16 SERVINGS.

¾ pound cooked beef tongue
4¾ cups shredded frozen suet (see note)
4½ cups currants
¼ cup brown sugar
3 tablespoons candied orange peel
Shredded rind of 1 lemon

1 tablespoon ground cloves
1 tablespoon ground mace
2 teaspoons salt, or to taste
2 tablespoons verjuice (see note)
¼ cup white wine or sherry

Preheat the oven to 350°F.

Shred or mince the tongue. Combine it with the suet, currants, sugar, orange rind, lemon, spices, salt, verjuice, and wine. Put the mincemeat in a heavy baking pan, cover tightly, and bake 45 minutes. Cook, then use in pies or freeze for later use. This type of mincemeat must be cooked first or the suet will spoil.

For use in pies, preheat the oven to 400°F. while the oven is warming, line two 9-inch pie plates with short crust and fill with the mincemeat. Cover with a top crust and ornament with pastry figures as I have done on the pie shown on page 43. Brush with cold water and scatter granulated sugar over them. Bake in the preheated oven for 10 minutes, then reduce the heat to 350°F and continue baking for 35 minutes. Serve hot or cold. If you want to be very authentic, sprinkle brandy on the crust and set it ablaze as you bring the pies into the dining room. Miss Leslie will roll over in her grave!

NOTE: The suet used in cookery is not the same reeking fat sold by our butchers as winter bird food. First class suet is white, snow white, because it is fresh and comes from the loin. Reject any suet that is tinged with blood, gray spots, or has an off odor. You must pick the suet free of all membranes before using it. Suet spoils very quickly, so either process it or freeze it until you need it.

Shredding suet for mincemeat the old way was a nightmare. I can easily see why the dish commanded so much respect. Today, this step is simple. After picking the suet free of membranes, freeze it for 24 hours. Then process it in a food processor *without thawing it.* Use the pulse key and process until the suet acquires the texture of fluffy snow. It is then ready to use. Measure what you need immediately. Refreeze the rest.

Verjuice is the sour juice pressed from unripe grapes or crab apples. If lightly salted, it will ferment into a vinegar that retains much of the astringency of the fresh liquid. Lemon juice is often substituted, but it is not the same thing. I have used at various times both crab apple verjuice and green currant verjuice. If you cannot make your own verjuice, use vinegar.

SOURCE: *The Compleat Cook* (London: Printed by E. Tyler, 1658), 74.

London-born Frederick B. Atmore (1815–1879) established one of the most famous mincemeat and plum pudding businesses in the United States during the nineteenth century. (Roughwood Collection)

STEAMED FRUIT PUDDING

1887

YIELD: 8 TO 10 SERVINGS.

1 cup finely shredded suet (page 179)
1 cup brown sugar
¾ cup raisins
¾ cup currants
⅓ cup chopped citron

2½ cups all-purpose flour
½ teaspoon salt
1½ teaspoons baking powder
1½ cups extra-strong hot coffee

*B*ring water to a boil in a large vegetable steamer. Mix the suet, sugar, raisins, currants, and citron. Sift the flour, salt, and baking powder together twice, then combine with the other ingedients. Make a valley in the center, add the hot coffee and work this up into a stiff batter.

Soak a pudding bag in warm water, wring it out, and dust the inside with flour. Fill the bag with the batter and tie it tight, leaving only enough room for the pudding to expand as it cooks. Set the filled pudding bag on a rack in the vegetable steamer, cover, and steam 2 hours.

To serve, turn the pudding out on a platter and send it to the table with the sugar sauce suggested below.

China pudding bucket for steamed puddings, German, circa 1890.

HOT SAUCE FOR STEAMED FRUIT PUDDING

YIELD: 2½ CUPS.

¾ cup sugar
2 cups hot water
2 tablespoons all-purpose flour

1 tablespoon butter
2 teaspoons vanilla extract

Dissolve the sugar in the hot water over a low heat. Work the flour and butter to a paste, then add to the syrup. Whisk continuously and bring the sauce to a gentle boil. As soon as it thickens, remove from the heat and add the vanilla. Serve at once with the steamed pudding.

NOTE: This is a sufficient quantity of sauce for the above pudding

SOURCE: *The Hamburg Item* (Hamburg, Pa.), 20 July 1887.

Sugar Ornaments and Edible Toys

Cousin Madge's dark eyes were glistening with cheer: "Sweet like pound cake," she said, "sour like cranberry-tarts, everything is just right, and looks right."[1] Madge had just stolen a peek at the Christmas tree decorations in Nellie Eyster's 1865 children's novel *Sunny Hours,* and the scene looked very much like the picture on the following page, where mother is trimming a small tree set upon a table. To the wild delight of the children in the house, she is decorating the tree with good things to eat: white sugar cookies and crullers in the shape of animals, jumbles—the cookies shaped like rings—cherries made of red sugarwork, and small baskets of confectionery.

The coming of the Christmas tree and its gradual evolution from a small tabletop centerpiece to a floor-standing bush, greatly expanded culinary possibilities for the Christmas cook. Since the tree introduced the need to decorate, and new and interesting accents were always wanted, it encouraged American cooks to experiment and improvise from year to year.

The decades between 1855 and 1875 witnessed a remarkable explosion in the variety of foods appropriated for use as tree decorations, but the greatest change took place in confectionery. The industrialization of candymaking had much to do with it. New methods of processing brought down the price of sugar and made the best grades of

Clear-toy candies from nineteenth-century molds.
(Courtesy of Charles Regennas, Lititz, Pennsylvania)

Frontispiece of *The Pictorial Scrap Book* (1860).
(Roughwood Collection)

white sugar, formerly a luxury, available to large numbers of people.

The mass production of such decorative items as scrap pictures, tinsel papers, and paper cornucopias encouraged the development of a specialized department of the confectionery industry specifically devoted to Christmas. After the consolidation of Germany into one country in 1871, a number of American confectioners took advantage of favorable trade laws to import huge quan-

tities of Christmas goods from Germany.[2] This shift is very easy to follow in issues of *The Confectioners' Journal* during the last quarter of the nineteenth century.

Between 1872 and 1906, when import laws were changed, American confectionery shops brimmed each Christmas with inexpensive German goods. It is probably safe to say that during the second half of the nineteenth century, more confectionery ended up on American Christmas trees than at any other time in our history, especially if we take into account the popularity of such things as nougat baskets, spun sugar birds' nests (for marzipan eggs and birds), and the general use of paper cornucopias to hold bounties of bonbons and candies.

The nougat baskets, the birds' nests, the log cabins of brown candy, the blown sugar vases and fruit, these were the products of professional candymakers. Outside of large cities, their availability was limited, and they were expensive everywhere. On the other hand, cornucopias could be made at home, and many paper companies issued designs that could be bought flat and folded together later. Thus, the cornucopia became one of the most common ways to hang confectionery on the tree.

Millions of cornucopias were made each year, but since they were meant to be thrown away, very few have survived from the nineteenth century to give us some idea of how they looked. This is a research question of great interest to the many people who want to reconstruct period Christmas trees.

In fact, the demand has been considerable enough to encourage some paper and card firms to revive Victorian cornucopia patterns, but very few that I have seen equal the eye-catching beauty of the old designs.

Some time ago, I discovered a rare illustrated advertisement for a handsome ready-made cornucopia issued in 1878 by the firm of Cornell & Shelton of Birmingham, Connecticut.[3] This pattern was printed in various colors of ink on shaded or metallic paper, for example, dark blue on gold brocade or violet on pale rose. The wonderful colors used on the old cornucopias sometimes show up in unexpected places, as for example, in the 1870s trade card of the Philadelphia chocolate maker Croft, Wilbur & Company on page 187.

Here, a festive green and gold cornucopia is spilling forth bonbons as though it were the gondola of a balloon. The colonial-revival garb of the children is meant to suggest a colonial—and therefore "old traditional"—connection with the firm's Christmas products.

This looking backward to a more golden Christmas past becomes an overriding concern for late Victorians. Industrialization, the decline of the farmer, massive immigration from eastern and southern Europe, all of these factors contributed in their own way to a new search for an American identity. One of the side effects of this was a renewal of interest in heirloom Christmas recipes. The 1880s and 1890s abound with nostalgic accounts of how things were done in the good old days.

Housekeeper's Weekly for December 1892, for example, described many of the old-fashioned bonbons that mothers and grandmothers had put on trees years before: coconut bars, hickory nut macaroons, vanilla cream

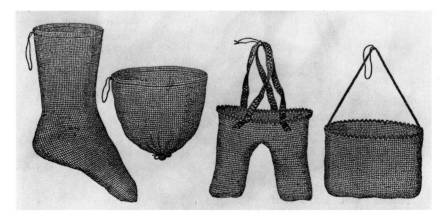

Woven bonbonniers of silver, blue, and rose tinsel for hanging confections on the Christmas tree. From a 1909 catalogue advertisement.
(Roughwood Collection)

Sugar Ornaments and Edible Toys

A Cornell & Shelton cornucopia from an 1878 advertisement in *The Confectioners' Journal.*

candy, fondant, chocolate creams, fruit balls, glacé fruits, and nuts.[4]

To be sure, such recipes were all somewhat time-consuming and in those days not easy to carry off unless one possessed a decent iron cookstove and copper pans. What the article in *Housekeeper's Weekly* did not mention was that most of those confections originated not as a branch of home cookery but in the hands of professional confectioners. In short, during the seventeenth, eighteenth, and nineteenth centuries, home cookery gradually adapted professional confectionery recipes and simplified them. In the process, home cooks sometimes created new and interesting variations.

The oldest home confections connected with Christmas included the various fruit pastes that could be molded or shaped into figures. Marmalade of Quinces (page 204) was one of the most common, marmalade in this case cooked down until it is stiff. While warm, it can be worked into shapes—the jumble or ring shape was very popular in colonial America. Beet Butter (page 209) and Raisiné (page 212), made with raisins and wine, were stiff marmalades made on the same principle as the quince. They could be molded into cherries, hearts, and other small shapes to be hung on the tree or piled with glacé fruits into fanciful towers on the Christmas *ambigue,* or buffet. Because it was black, raisiné was often used as an imitation of truffle garnishing, as I have done on the capon of Lemon and Rum Jelly in chapter 8.

Of all the Christmas confections, the clear toy or barley sugar candy has remained the least changed over the past 300 years. Granted, it was a confectioner's art insofar as barley sugar required molds, and mass production is what makes clear toys cheap, but anyone could make this candy at home if he wanted to. And for molds, any home cook could make them with a little plaster of paris and sculptural ingenuity—realizing, of course, that one must carve all designs in reverse. Oftentimes, cooks had no choice but to use their native ingenuity, especially when home was in the country far from city shops and confectioners.

Chromolithograph trade card, circa 1876. (Roughwood Collection)

Because of the rarity of clear-toy recipes in household cookbooks prior to the eighteenth century, I was surprised to discover in the 1638 manuscript cookbook of Lettice Arnold of Herfordshire, England, a recipe called "To make anie Artifitiall fruits" using three-part alabaster molds—what we today call plaster of paris.[5] Lettice made pippins (apples), oranges, lemons, and cucumbers with her molds, using saffron for the lemons and a vibrant color called "Sapp green," which she bought from the apothecary, for the cucumbers.

Lettice Arnold was a gentlewoman in the truest Elizabethan sense, and doubtless time-consuming sugarwork of that sort was considered a necessary part of her feminine training as a person of title and heiress to many large estates. It was an exacting and taxing test at that, considering that in the seventeenth and eighteenth centuries sugarwork was prepared in brass or copper pans over charcoal stoves.

Not many cookbooks today contain recipes for making clear toys, even though the procedure is simplicity itself. The main reason, I think, is that most people today do not own the type of metal molds that have been used by candy makers since the 1860s.

Elaborate molds of the traditional kind, the sort I have used in testing my recipe, are of course a problem for those who do not

A copper saucepan, for small batches of candy, was set over hot charcoal in a chafing dish as shown here. The perforated pewter spoon was used to test the various stages of sugar. All utensils pictured date from about 1700–1715.

The Christmas Cook

4 cups sugar
1 cup water
¼ teaspoon cream of tartar

Green, red, or yellow food coloring
Lemon extract (optional)

Dissolve the sugar, water, and cream of tartar. Do not stir once the syrup begins to boil. Boil hard to just slightly beyond the hard crack stage (325°F), which should take about 15 minutes. Add coloring and lemon flavor if you choose, stirring quickly two or three times. Pour the syrup into molds that must be wired shut so that they do not accidentally pop open. Do not use rubber bands; they will melt.

The sugar will foam up when poured into the metal molds, so be extremely careful about splattering. Pour slowly, a little at a time, but pour steadily. Should you prefer not to use molds, then pour large drops of syrup onto clean metal baking sheets. The drops will harden into medallions. Or, as the sugar cools, pull it quickly into shapes like glass animals.

NOTE: If left too long in the molds, the candy will shatter when you try to remove it. On the other hand, if the sugar is still too warm, the figure will pull or stretch when the mold is opened. There is a critical point when the candy is ready; it varies almost from mold to mold and is knowledge that must be acquired through trial and error. As soon as the candy is removed from the mold, trim off the rough spots with a sharp knife, done very carefully, of course, so that no scars are visible.

SOURCE: Priscilla Homespun, pseud., *The Universal Receipt Book* (Philadelphia: Isaac Riley, 1818), 177.

Sugar Ornaments and Edible Toys

CANDIED ORANGE OR LEMON PEEL

1801

Under an article called "Two Old Recipes" in the *Confectioner and Baker* for April 1901, the editor remarked that there were some old-time recipes that could not be improved upon. One of these, a confection rarely seen at the time, was candied orange peel. Evidently, by 1900, it had given way to a myriad of more elaborate things. Yet, as he remarked: "placed in a dainty box lined with silk paper, this dainty confection is most acceptable."[9]

I have tried many recipes for candying lemon and orange peel, but none of them—even the one cited in the *Confectioner and Baker*—are as fail-safe as the method given by Elizabeth Raffald. While her recipe may look complicated, it is actually quite simple, and the results are always good. Best of all, the leftover syrup can be used to make orange granité, an orange-flavored slush that can be served like Yule Tide Punch. Or, add a little orange curaçao or rum and you will have a perfect *coupe de milieu* for your Christmas dinner.

YIELD: AT LEAST 1 POUND CANDIED PEEL.

10 oranges (see note) or 15 lemons
2 quarts plus 1 cup spring water or
bottled water (see note)
2 tablespoons pickling salt or kosher salt

4 cups granulated sugar
Superfine sugar

Remove the rinds from the oranges or lemons and cut them into halves or quarters. Reserve the fruit sections of the oranges for Orange Granité (page 206). Bring 1 quart spring water and the pickling salt to a boil. Boil hard for 5 minutes. Set aside to cool. When cool, pour into a large jar, add the rinds, cover, and store in the refrigerator for 6 days. After 6 days, pour the brine into a preserving kettle and bring to a hard boil. Reduce the heat, add the rinds, and *poach* for 10 minutes. Drain the rinds thoroughly in a colander and discard the brine.

Clean the preserving kettle and make a syrup in it with 1 quart spring water and 2 cups sugar. Bring this to a hard boil, then add the rinds and boil hard for about 30 minutes, or until the peels begin to look clear around the edges. Remove the rinds with a skimmer or slotted spoon and drain them in a colander. Reserve the syrup for Orange Granité.

Clean the preserving kettle and make a syrup in it with the remaining 1 cup spring water and 2 cups sugar. Bring this to a hard boil. Cut the rinds into strips and put them in the boiling syrup. Let this boil gently until the syrup candies on the strips. remove the strips and spread them to dry on racks. Drying time will vary with weather conditions. Allow at least 1 day. When the strips are dry, dust them lightly with superfine sugar and store in airtight containers.

NOTE: The best oranges for this purpose are thick-skinned dessert oranges, preferably California oranges. If you are fortunate enough to find small Spanish blood oranges, this recipe will candy the rinds of about 20.

It is imperative that you do *not* use tap water for this recipe. The chemical additives in common drinking water will cause the confection to deteriorate.

SOURCE: Elizabeth Raffald, *The Experienced English Housekeeper* (Philadelphia: Printed for Thomas Dobson, 1801), 206.

Christmas card issued by Philadelphia toy store owner, G. A. Schwarz, 1881. (Roughwood Collection)

GLACÉ FRUITS

Huling's recipe calls for double the amounts given here, which would require at least 2 persons working together quickly to get it all done before the sugar sets. Keep that in mind if you are working alone. It is far better to do a smaller batch twice than to have large amounts of sugar gone hard before you are half finished. Otherwise, this is very easy to do and quite spectacular when used on fruit pyramids and fancy Christmas centerpieces in combination with candles.

YIELD: SUFFICIENT FOR 5 TO 6 POUNDS OF FRUIT.

4 cups sugar
1 cup water

¼ teaspoon cream of tartar

Put the sugar, water, and cream of tartar in a preserving pan and stir over high heat until the sugar is dissolved. Do not stir the syrup when it begins to boil. Boil hard until it reaches the hard crack stage (325°F), then remove from the heat and set the pan on a work table. Dip the lightest colored fruit first, the darker fruits as the syrup begins to darken. Reheat the sugar if necessary to keep it fluid. Drain and dry the dipped fruit on wire racks. Set away in paper cases as soon as the sugar is hard. Use paper cases of different colors like the ones used for fancy chocolates. They may be purchased in stores specializing in culinary equipment.

NOTE: When using fresh fruit, it is probably best to do a small test run first because boiling sugar sometimes discolors thin-skinned fruits, especially pears. It is a good idea to know what will happen before committing a large amount of work to a full batch.

Also, glacé fruits, unless made with dried fruits, will not keep for a long period of time. In fact, I would only allow 2 days in cool weather. If you plan to do a pyramid of fruit, such as the small one on page 235, do it in the morning on the day of the party. If problems develop, you will then have time to make last-minute repairs.

Some suggested fruits and nuts:

Red and white preserved pears, cut in quarters
Greengage plums, cut in half and seeded
Dried or fresh apricots
Fresh limes, chosen for brightness of color
Pineapple slices and chunks, fresh or candied
Shelled, cooked chestnuts
Fresh cherries with stems
Dried or fresh figs

SOURCE: Charles Huling, *Revised American Candy Maker* (Philadelphia: Privately published, 1908), 258.

POTATO FONDANT

1914

If you intend to sculpt fruits or other figures in imitation of marzipan, it is pointless to make a smaller quantity than that given here. If you want to use the fondant as a filling for small bonbons, reduce the recipe by half.

YIELD: APPROXIMATELY 6 POUNDS OF FONDANT.

1 pound white potatoes, cooked and mashed (2 cups)
4 egg whites

5 pounds confectioners' sugar (about 20 cups)
Oil of bitter almond (optional)

After the potatoes are pared, it is best to steam them until soft rather than boil them. This will reduce excess moisture. Force the potatoes through a sieve, colander, or potato ricer, then measure out 2 cups. For each ½ cup of potato, you must allow 1 egg white.

When the mashed potatoes are cool, work in the egg whites with a large spoon, but do not beat the mixture. Gradually sift in the confectioners' sugar until the fondant becomes stiff and does not adhere to the hands. Put the fondant on a cold marble slab and knead it like bread dough until it becomes pliant, about 20 to 30 minutes. Then put it in a bowl and cover. Store in the refrigerator until needed.

Take out only what is required for immediate use, and shape it as you would marzipan. Additional confectioners' sugar can be worked into the fondant to give it a pastry-like consistency for rolling out and cutting into shapes, such as leaves and other applied decorations similar to *pâté d'office*. Or, mold it into freeform figures, like the leaves and roses on the Twelfth Night Cake shown on page 4.

NOTE: When using this fondant with molds similar to those used with Springerle dough or paste sugar, you will get better results by brushing each mold very lightly with olive oil. The fondant will then pull away perfectly. If it should look "wet," however, this is an indication that you have been too liberal with the olive oil.

This fondant will dry fairly quickly when left in the open, provided the air is cool and the humidity low. In humid weather, it is preferable to work in an air-conditioned room.

SOURCE: Mary Elizabeth Hall, *Candy Making Revolutionized* (New York: Sturgis and Walton, 1914), 61–66.

During the eighteenth and nineteenth centuries, pulled taffy was a popular American street food. It was not as creamy white as this recipe because it was often made with molasses, but it was white enough to pass in folk judgment under several suggestive names. In Pennsylvania, the candy was called "bellyguts"; in New York, it was called "cock-a-nee-nee." Both were considered vulgar, which of course endeared the candies all the more to the children who hawked them—and ate them.

Gradually, bellyguts and its various cousins became nostalgically associated with the pre–Civil War period and by degrees connected more and more with Christmas. By the time Mrs. Frances Owens published her popular *Cook Book and Useful Household Hints* in 1884, the shift was complete. Her recipe is simply called "Christmas Candy." [14]

I have gone to another authority for my recipe, however: Sarah Tyson Rorer. The reason is quite simple: her recipe is fail safe. And in this case, unlike barley sugar, gum arabic *is* necessary.

YIELD: 1 POUND CANDY.

1 teaspoon gum arabic
1 cup plus 1 tablespoon water
2 cups sugar

½ teaspoon cream of tartar (see note)
1 teaspoon vanilla extract

Dissolve the gum arabic in 1 tablespoon of water. Put the sugar, cream of tartar, 1 cup water, and dissolved gum arabic in a preserving pan and stir over high heat until the sugar is dissolved. Wipe the inside of the pan with a sponge (to prevent crystallization) and boil the syrup until it reaches a hard crack (325°F). Pour it out onto a greased glass platter or marble slab. When cool enough to handle (in roughly 5 minutes), add the flavoring and roll the candy up. Butter the hands and have *two persons* pull the taffy. Pull vigorously and continuously until perfectly white. Braid into a long stick. Cut into six-inch lengths and store in an airtight box. It must stand at least 2 hours before it is ready to eat.

Incidentally, when you braid the taffy, it should resemble the large intestine of a pig; that is how the term "bellyguts" originated.

NOTE: If you dissolve the gum arabic in 1 tablespoon of vinegar and omit the cream of tartar, the results will be the same. For a flavor similar to Christmas candy canes, use ten drops of peppermint oil instead of vanilla. Incidentally, gum arabic is generally available from druggists or chemical supply houses. Some herb shops, like Aphrodisia in New York City, stock it regularly and are willing to ship to mail order customers.

SOURCE: Sarah Tyson Rorer, *Home Candy Making* (Philadelphia: Arnold & Co., 1886), 58–59.

Chromolithograph trade cards, circa 1875. Bellyguts are shown in the card above. (Roughwood Collection)

CONFECTIONERS' PASTE

1849

*T*his is also commonly known as *pâté d'office*. As the original recipe we are using stated: "From this paste may be made cottages, temples, fountains, pyramids, castles, bridges, hermits' cells, vases, or any other required forms, which are to be made in different pieces and put together afterwards or formed in moulds, and either baked or dried out in the stove."[10] The forms referred to were called *pièces montées*, monumental centerpieces for the festive table that were popular right down to the turn of this century. The sugarwork gazebo shown in the center of the table on pages 202–203 required about 10 to 12 pounds of paste.

Gum tragacanth (*Astragalus gummifer*), also called "gum dragon," was often used as an ingredient in confectioners' paste instead of egg whites. It was considered by many confectioners even superier to egg white or gum arabic as a stiffening agent. The gum was extracted from a thorny bush native to the Near East. In the nineteenth century, most gum tragacanth was imported to this country from Turkey.[11] At that time, it was available from even the smallest apothecary shops, but today it is almost impossible to buy except through wholesale suppliers. For this reason, I have avoided using it.

YIELD: 2½ POUNDS PASTE.

5¾ cups pastry flour
1⅓ cups superfine sugar

8 egg whites

*S*ift 5¼ cups of flour and all the sugar together in a large work bowl. Form a valley in the center and add the egg whites. Stir and combine until a sticky dough is formed. Then add the remaining ½ cup flour and knead the dough until soft and spongy like bread dough. Cover and set away in the refrigerator to ripen overnight.

Break off only what is needed. When using intricate molds, such as the one shown on page 57, dust it lightly with a brush dipped in flour. Blow away any excess flour. Roll out the paste to the desired thickness on

a work surface (a marble slab is best) lightly dusted with flour. Then press the mold into it. Lift the mold away and cut out the figures with a sharp knife or Exacto blade. Or, cut out the figure after it is half baked or dried in the oven. Then return it to the oven to finish. Either way, it is a good idea to lightly grease your baking sheets to ensure that your handiwork does not stick. I prefer to use baking parchment.

Small figures should be dried in a slack oven prehated to 175°F; larger pieces may be baked in an oven preheated to 275°F or

325°F, depending on size and thickness. There is no set rule here, except the more delicate the piece, the lower the oven temperature. Your only object is to dehydrate and stiffen the dough while maintaining its white color and ornamental shape. Usually, 10 to 15 minutes are long enough. All pieces are "done" when they are thoroughly hard and dry. Let them cool on racks before assembling.

Your paste may be colored or even marbelized when you first mix it. Any colored or marbelized pastes should be dried out slowly at 175°F rather than baked; higher temperatures often cause colors to turn.

Once your pieces are cool, glue them together with carmelized sugar (or real glue if you do not intend to eat your masterpiece). You may further ornament a pièce montée as the Victorians did with spun sugar or with colored granulated sugars. This recipe was used to make the cherub figure on the Twelfth Night Cake pictured on page 4.

SOURCE: James W. Parkinson, ed., *The Complete Confectioner* (Philadelphia: Leary & Getz, 1849), 89.

Tin cutters for paste sugar ornaments, 1870s.

Sugar Ornaments and Edible Toys

The centerpiece for this abundant dessert setting is a pièce
montée temple of paste sugar. From an 1873 chromolithograph
book illustration. (Roughwood Collection)

*T*his recipe makes what the medieval French called *condoignac*, or in English *chardequynce* (meat of quince). It is taken from *The Family Companion*, the oldest known cookbook printed in America, and one which was evidently compiled by an American with an interest in viticulture, since there is a section on winemaking "of our own growth."

I cannot overstate the love colonial Americans had for quinces, a fruit that is now sadly all too rare on the market. I should add that this particular marmalade is not the same marmalade that we know today, but rather a marmalade cooked down to its natural conclusion. It is a stiffish paste that congeals into a "just Thickness," as the original recipe described it, soft, chewy, and very rich.

This is the texture of true marmalade as it was originally made in Portugal and exported to England in the 1500s.[12] The English word *marmalade* is derived from the Portuguese word for quince conserve: *marmelada*. This has led to valid speculation among food historians that the Portuguese confection made of honey and quinces, may have been known even in Roman times. If so, then it is indeed an old delight that made its way into Christmas cookery at an extremely early date.

YIELD: APPROXIMATELY 2 DOZEN
2-INCH JUMBLES.

1 pound quinces (approximately 5 quinces), weight after paring and coring
2 cups granulated sugar

Zest of 1 lemon
Superfine sugar

*P*reheat the oven to 350°F.

Pare and core the quinces, cut them into large pieces, and weigh. You must begin with 1 pound of fruit.

Set the quinces in a deep pot without water and cover tight. Bake for approximately 40 to 50 minutes, or until soft. *Do not scorch the fruit.* Purée the fruit to a fine paste in a food processor, blender, or the old way, by passing the fruit through a fine sieve. The paste must be perfectly smooth and without lumps. Now weigh the paste to be certain that you still have 1 pound of fruit.

To each pound of paste, add 2 cups of granulated sugar and the grated zest of 1 lemon. Put the mixture into a preserving pan and boil it hard for approximately 20 minutes, or until it becomes thick and ropy. At this point, the marmalade should pull away from the pan in a large ball when stirred with a spoon.

Spread the marmalade as quickly as possible on glass pans or platters and let it cool. The normal thickness preferred in most old recipes is ¼ inch.

When cool, the marmalade should stiffen into a doughlike consistency. Cut it in 5-inch strips and connect the strips to make rings. Roll the rings in superfine sugar and ley them between wax paper in airtight containers. I have used jumbles or rings made in this manner in the photograph on page xvi.

NOTE: Do not attempt to make more than a 1-pound batch at a time or you will probably burn the bottom before you cook the top. Any scorching of the fruit or marmalade will destroy the delicate flavor.

Historically, the most common way to present marmalade candy was to cut it into lozenge shapes and roll these in fine sugar as shown on page 74. I have chosen the ring or jumble because this was also a traditional shape, and one closely associated with early Christmas tree decoration, as so often seen in old illustrations.

Mrs. Howland, in her *American Economical Housekeeper* (1850 edition), used brown sugar instead of white, a common adaptation in rural households where white sugar was simply too expensive even for Christmas feasting.[13] Common quince marmalade turns an attractive rose-pink when properly cooked and the quinces well-chosen for ripeness. Brown sugar, however, makes brown marmalade. For a handsome array of subtle colors, do a batch of marmalade "natural," another batch tinted with beet juice, another tinted with saffron, and one made with brown sugar. When cast in sheets in shallow Pyrex baking trays, the marmalades can be cut up into shapes and used as inlay work on iced cakes or as garnishings on small pastries.

Apples can be used in this recipe instead of quinces, but the flavor is not the same, nor is the texture, due to less pectin. For a related recipe using apples, see the recipe for Gâteau de Pommes in chapter 8.

SOURCE: *The Secretary's Guide, or Young Man's Companion . . . to Which Is Added the Family Companion.* (Philadelphia: Printed for Andrew Bradford, 1737), 235. Quoted with the permission of the Historical Society of Pennsylvania.

Sugar Ornaments and Edible Toys

ORANGE GRANITÉ

— 1893 —

YIELD: 8 TO 10 SERVINGS.

2 cups sugar
1 quart spring water or
Reserved syrup from recipe for Candied Orange
or Lemon Peel (page 194)

1 pint freshly squeezed orange juice
(juice of about 6 oranges, or use
orange sections reserved from Candied
Orange or Lemon Peel)

Boil the sugar and spring water or reserved syrup hard for 5 minutes, then let it cool. Strain the orange juice and add this to the cooled syrup. Pour into a clean metal container, cover tightly, and freeze. When frozen to a slush consistency, beat it with a whisk to get out any lumps. Serve in ice cream glasses and garnish with slices of fresh orange.

SOURCE: *Table Talk* 8 (September 1893), 325.

PEANUT TAFFY

1870

The oldest method for making this type of hard taffy, which can be traced at least to the eighteenth century, was to pour it into small molds or pattypans. In Europe, almonds were most commonly used, although hazelnuts and walnuts were also popular. In America, peanuts were often substituted for more expensive imported nuts. Like belly-guts, described in Old-Fashioned Cream Candy, peanut candy was also hawked in the streets.

YIELD: APPROXIMATELY 1 POUND OF CANDY.

1 cup brown sugar
¼ cup water

4 tablespoons butter
2 cups toasted unsalted shelled peanuts

*P*ut the sugar and water in a saucepan and boil until the sugar is dissolved and becomes dark and clear. Then add the butter. Stir until the buter melts, then boil hard for 15 minutes or until the syrup reaches the hard crack stage (325°F). Add peanuts, stir and remove from the heat. Spread the candy on buttered baking sheets or press into buttered tin pattypans. When the candy begins to harden, cut it into squares or diamonds with a sharp knife dipped in water. Or, once hard, break up into irregular pieces. This makes what we now call peanut brittle.

NOTE: The sugar must be fully dissolved before you begin to boil it hard, or it will recrystallize instead of forming taffy. Also, I have found that while it is not always necessary, it is adviseable to heat the peanuts in an oven preset to 325°F for 5 minutes before mixing them with the taffy. If the nuts are much cooler than the boiling sugar, they may cause it to harden prematurely.

SOURCE: *The Queen of the Kitchen: A Collection of Old Maryland Recipes for Cooking* (Baltimore: Lucas Brothers, 1870), 234.

Tin candy pans for Peanut Taffy, circa 1830.

Tin molds for Beet Butter, circa 1850.

BEET BUTTER

This confection is particularly well adapted for molding into cherries and hearts for the Christmas tree.

YIELD: 2 POUNDS OF CONFECTION.

1 pound beets
2 cups sugar
2 tablespoons lemon juice
¼ teaspoon ground cinnamon
¼ teaspoon grated nutmeg

Wash the beets thoroughly, then place them in a pan with sufficient water to cover. Bring to a boil and cook until the beets are tender (cooking time will depend on the size of the beets). Reserve the cooking liquid for soup. Rinse the beets under cold water and remove the skins.

Purée the beets as fine as possible using a little of the cooking liquid if necessary. Re-weigh the purée to be certain there is one pound. The weight of the beet purée and sugar must be equal.

Mix the beet purée with the sugar and lemon juice. Bring this to a hard boil in a preserving pan and boil for 20 minutes. Add the cinnamon and nutmeg. Stir continuously and boil for another 5 to 8 minutes, or until the confection lifts from the bottom of the pan in a ball around the spoon.

Spread it immediately on glass platters to cool so that it can be handled. When it is still warm, but not so hot as to burn the fingers, press the paste into candy molds and let it cool. If the candy is to be hung as a Christmas tree decoration, insert small wires or strings into the back of each piece. When set, remove from the molds and store in airtight containers.

NOTE: Depending on the material your molds are made of, you will have varying success in removing the candy from the forms. Tinned copper seems to work remarkably well; china or porcelain work best of all. Some confectioners brushed the insides of their molds very lightly with water or olive oil. This often alleviates the problem of sticking. Also, use a very sharp knife dipped in water to go around the inside edge of each form. This will help to loosen the candy, which should then pull out without much trouble.

SOURCE: George Girardey, *Höchst nützliches Handbuch über Kochkunst* (Cincinnati: J. A. James, 1842), 164–65.

MARZIPAN

1804

YIELD: 1 POUND MARZIPAN.

8 ounces blanched almonds
1 cup superfine sugar

8 tablespoons rosewater

*P*reheat the oven to 170°F.

In a blender or food processor using the metal blade, work the almonds with the sugar, adding the rosewater a little at a time, until a thick, smooth paste forms. Spread the paste on a baking sheet and dry it out in a slack oven (170°F) until the paste acquires a doughlike consistency. Stamp with wooden marzipan molds or shape into figures as you would sculptor's putty, then dry out again in the slack oven. When the surface of the marzipan is dry, paint it with food coloring or colored sugar icing.

NOTE: If you plan to make marzipan on a regular basis, you may want to invest in sculpting tools of the sort available from art supply shops. Historically, confectioners had special tools made of horn or ivory for shaping marzipan. In the 1920s and 1930s, these tools were available in celluloid but are now no longer made in this country. Today wooden copies made in Taiwan can sometimes be found in art supply stores.

SOURCE: Neues Gothaisches Kochbuch, Part 2 (Gotha: Ettingerschen Buchhandlung, 1804), 267–68.

Tools for sculpting marzipan as illustrated in James Parkinson's *The Complete Confectioner* (1849). Beside them, a marzipan crab apple and a gilded marzipan urn of flowers.

RAISINÉ

This recipe, also known as "raisin cheese," comes from a clipping in the manuscript cookbook of Mary H. Winebrenner, second wife of Reverend John Winebrenner, founder of the Church of God in 1820. Mrs. Winebrenner was well known throughout the middle states for her culinary accomplishments. And like her recipe for Gâteau de Pommes in the next chapter, this one certainly indicates a level of ability far above the average, one verging in fact on the professional. Of course, this kind of training was often expected of the wives of leading ministers, since they were responsible for their husband's constant flow of visitors and religious dignitaries. It is no wonder, then, that Mrs. Winebrenner's notebook is also full of Christmas recipes. Christmas must have been her busiest time of year.

YIELD: APPROXIMATELY 3½ TO 4 POUNDS OF CONFECTION.

1½ pounds cooking apples (about 6 large apples), weight after paring and coring
1 cup sugar

4 tablespoons Madeira
2½ pounds raisins
2 to 2½ cups water

Stew the apples, sugar and Madeira in a heavy saucepan until the apples are soft. Purée the mixture thoroughly to remove all lumps. Return it to the cooking vessel and add the raisins and just enough water to keep the mixture from burning, about 2 cups. Stew until the raisins are completely soft, adding water from time to time, if necessary.

Purée the entire batch as fine as possible, then put it into a preserving kettle.

Bring the purée to a hard boil and reduce until thick, stirring constantly to keep it from scorching. When the raisiné lifts from the pan in a ropy ball, it is ready to pour into molds. Or, spread it ¼ inch thick on glass baking dishes and allow it to cool. This can then be sliced as ornamentation for pastry or confections, or cut into shapes with small tin cutters. Store in airtight containers between sheets of wax paper, or freeze. This is meant to be used as a garnish, not eaten like marmalade—it is far too rich.

NOTE: In order to get the correct consistency, you must cook the purée almost to the point when you think you are about to burn it. This may seem a bit tricky at first, but once you do it, the finish point becomes easy to recognize because the confection develops a ropy quality that pulls on the spoon. You can feel the change as you are stirring.

SOURCE: Mary Hamilton Winebrenner, "Housekeeper's Book" manuscript cookbook (Harrisburg, Pa.: 1837–1879). Roughwood Collection.

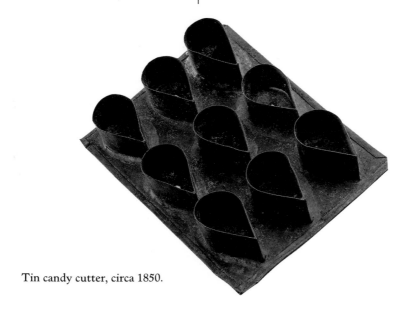

Tin candy cutter, circa 1850.

EIGHT

Kisses at the End

*N*ow that we have explored the various departments of Christmas cookery—the cookies, the cakes, the puddings, and sugarwork—it is time to focus our attention on the larger picture: How to put it all together for the Christmas table. What I have in mind is an arrangement of foods buffet-style, or as it was called in the eighteenth century, an *ambigue*.

An ambigue begins with a centerpiece, and then around it we lay out plates and dishes of various shapes and heights in a geometric plan. For example, we place identical round dishes on each corner of the table (assuming the table is rectangular); four oval platters, one on the middle of each side; and four glass stands at each corner of the centerpiece. This is a bit sketchy and quite simple by old-time standards, but at least it gives you a general idea of what we are talking about. There is of course a linen tablecloth beneath the service ware, and some of the space between dishes and platters is filled with evergreens, dried flowers, fruits, and confectionery. Candelabra are stationed at critical places in the arrangement to throw light on the food in an inviting manner.

Glass salvers await guests at "early candlelight" (dusk). On the left, the tiers of Iced Grapes, Chocolate Apeas, Zephyr Cookies, and Little Plumcakes (PAGE 128); and Gooseberry and Vanilla Creams garnished with red currants are crowned with a topiary wreath of gooseberry geranium and St. Nicholas cookie. On the table below, a Gâteau de Pommes ornamented with almond slivers (PAGES 226–227). On the stand to the right, a Clear Toy sailing ship is surrounded by Brandy Snaps (PAGE 137).

From Charles Carter's *The Complete Practical Cook*
(1730). (Roughwood Collection)

For large ambigues, such as those illustrated in Charles Carter's *Complete Practical Cook* of 1730, the dinner plates for the guests were stacked around the outer edge of the arrangement. His ambigue for a masquerade is shown above. You are looking down on the table plan as though suspended from the chandeliers overhead.

You will note that in the center there is a pyramid of sweetmeats and fruit in porcelain dishes. Carter has also mixed the meat dishes —salmon, cold turkey, collared pig—the pies, and the desserts together on the same table, which is proper for an ambigue because the term implies that there are no separate courses in the meal. It is a dinner served according to the French term *á l'ambigue,* meaning "ambiguous style," no particular order of courses.

In colonial America, only the governors of the various colonies and the wealthiest citizens served their meals in this highly ornamental manner. But many festive dinners, even when scaled down to the modest means of a farmhouse table, echoed this arrangement in one way or another. Very often, rather than an ambigue with meats and sweets mixed, the table was laid out with desserts alone, which was quite popular, especially for New Years and Twelfth Night entertainments.

PYRAMIDS AND PIÈCES MONTÉES

This family of centerpieces falls into five broad categories.

Moravian *Leuchterstand* or pyramid for evergreens, animal cookies, and decorative *Putz* (carved wooden figures). Copy of an eighteenth-century original.

The Christmas Cook

Wooden Pyramids

There is great variety in the types of designs used for these wooden structures, from simple affairs made of four short poles, teepee fashion, to "trees" with elaborate wood turnings and little cups to hold candles. The *Leuchterstand* pictured on page 217 is a type of pyramid known to have been made by the Moravians in Pennsylvania. It is constructed of 56 interlocking pieces of wood. There are no nails or pegs holding it together. A similar pyramid, dating from the eighteenth century, is in the Museum of Folk Art at Dresden, East Germany.

Cake tins for a pyramid of cakes, circa 1850.

Glass Stands Stacked into Towers

These are glass salvers or cake stands stacked sometimes three or four high, one on top of the other, and the various tiers or levels filled with such foods as Cranberry Tarts, Brandy Snaps, Nic-Nacs, and Iced Grapes. Iced Grapes were especially well liked because they could be draped over the edges. They give a wonderful snowy effect to the arrangement. There is a recipe for making Iced Grapes on page 237. A glass stand with Iced Grapes on two levels may be seen on page 214.

A Pyramid of Cakes

Lettice Bryan noted in *The Kentucky Housewife*:

A pyramid of cake is introduced only at the finest suppers. Make them all of common pound cake, or have every cake of a different quality, if you choose. The pans in which they are baked should all be of a circular form, gradually diminishing in circumference, from the largest to the smallest size. Ice them very white, and when they get about half dry, put round each a decorament of devices and borders in white sugar, or a very delicate garland or festoon. When the icing gets perfectly dry, stack them regularly, putting the largest at the bottom, and the smallest on the top, and stick a small bunch of real or artificial flowers on the pinnacle, or top cake.[1]

Between 1841, when this was written, and the 1890s, this type of cake shifted from party cake to wedding cake. As a wedding cake, it was a substitute for the more expensive pièce montée.

At the end Mrs. Bryan's recipe for Fruit Pound Cake in chapter 4, I have illustrated such a pyramid of cakes.

Sugarwork Pyramids and Pièces Montées

Catherine Beecher described a clever way to avoid the trouble of making a cake in her *The Handy Cook Book* of 1873. She boiled sugar to the candy stage and used it like paint to cover a large cone made of cardboard. The cardboard was first buttered, then "set it on the table, and begin at the bottom, and stick on this frame with the sugar, a row of macaroons, kisses, or other ornamental articles, and continue till the whole is covered. When cold, draw out the pasteboard form, and set the pyramid in the center of the table with a small bit of wax candle burning within . . . it looks very beautifully."[2] The glow is luminous, like a snow lantern.

Or, you may construct a pièce montée of paste sugar as described in chapter 7.

Pyramids of Small Popcorn Balls

Because they are light, popcorn balls can be constructed into very high pyramids held together with candied sugar and garnished with boxwood sprigs, red berries, and small dried flowers. These make attractive, tall cornerpieces and are inexpensive in terms of basic cost of materials. There is more about the history of popcorn on page 230.

SMALLER PYRAMIDS AND CORNERPIECES

Pyramids of more modest size can be constructed with many of the recipes included in this book. I would suggest glacé fruits, which are ideal for corner dishes or for elevating on low glass stands near candlelight. Also useful for this purpose are the recipes for peanut, almond, and hickory nut macaroons. Being lightweight, they can be stacked without crushing one another.

Individual glass stands may be used to call attention to certain decorative dishes, such as the Clear Toy sailing ship on page 214, a Gâteau de Pommes ornamented with almonds, Snow Balls, stacks of Chocolate Kisses, little piles of *Olie-Koecks,* molded puddings, Dutch Cake, and shallow pies like Pumpkin Pudding, which look very handsome when stationed above platters of dark-colored cookies.

Low fruit pieces are also well suited for the middle height areas of the table. One of the most impressive—yet easy to make—is the pyramid of oranges filled with two colors of gelatin featured on the cover of this book. The recipe is on pages 232–233.

OTHER CENTERPIECES

If you simply want something festive on the table that suggests Christmas without the grand display of dishes and desserts, you have many options. A gingerbread house is always fun. Humperdinck's opera *Hänsel and Gretel* did much to spread its popularity.[3] The gingerbread recipe on page 124 is well suited for this purpose, but roll it thicker than for small cookies.

Of course, you can have a great cake, like the Twelfth Night Cake on pages 20–21, ornamented with sugar or plaster figures. Or you can make a large Christmas "pie," like the one described in this 1916 account: "It was made in a cheese box, wrapped about with Christmas greens to conceal the box, the crust being made of brown paper, generously sprinkled with sugar. The crust was nicked enough to cut easily. And oh, the presents that came out of that blessed pie! Just the smaller gifts and favors. Dolls' tea sets and such things were made into many small packages; and there were nut and candy toys which were jokes on the grown-ups."[4]

You may also build yourself a Christmas pie (or gift pie—its other name) with the 1787 recipe for Crust for Raised Pies (page 99). But line it with wax paper before you fill it with little packages, or the crust will leave grease marks on the wrapping papers.

A simple punch bowl surrounded with plates of cookies can be highly ornamental if

Mold for making a gingerbread or sugarwork house, circa 1800–1850. (The Henry Francis DuPont Winterthur Museum)

care is taken to place evergreens and fruit around the base of the bowl. The recipe for Yule Tide Punch is perfect for this, yet it can also be adapted as a *coupe de milieu*, the middle course or pause, in dinner on Christmas Day. It is refreshing, but of a slushy consistency, and must therefore be served like a sorbet.

PLATEAUX

Plateaux, or mirrors with decorative borders raised on small feet, were popular additions to the festive table in the eighteenth and nineteenth centuries. They were quite expensive and easily broken. George Washington had one—a very large one—that he used for special occasions. His letters are full of fretful admonishments to his housekeepers over broken borders and little feet knocked in moving the plateau from house to house when he was President.

Despite their fragile nature, plateaux were considered worth the trouble because they reflected the light from nearby candelabras and overhead chandeliers, and thus gave the table a rare sparkle and elegance. Victorian plateaux were often small to accommodate small dining tables and middle-class incomes. The plateau from 1875 shown in the chromolithograph on page 239 is barely 24 inches from handle to handle. A large silver serving tray will make a perfectly suitable substitute, but polish it well.

The little syllabub glasses around the base of the bowl in this picture contain creams and jellies like those shown on page 214. I have provided you with a recipe for Orange Cream similar to the one called for in the picture. Cordial glasses may be used instead of syllabub glasses.

The Christmas tree as a table centerpiece, from *Peterson's Magazine*, December 1858. (Roughwood Collection)

The centerpiece, garnished with strips of candied fruit, dried flowers, and box greens, is none other than Snow Pudding, for which I have also provided the recipe. A tall glass candy dish can be appropriated to hold the pudding. To achieve that particular shape, make the pudding in a bowl that will fit inside the serving dish when turned upside down.

THE CHRISTMAS TREE

We now come to the most popular by far of all the Christmas centerpieces, the tabletop tree. No one today needs to be told how to erect such a tree, but there was a time when Christmas trees were not as well-known, and for that reason the following "recipe" was published in *The Farmer and Gardener* in December 1860:

> Cut off the top of a wild cedar-tree, and fasten securely in a keg or box (trimmed with cut paper) with saw dust, or earth and stones. Tie the gifts intended for the little ones—the wagons, drums and heavy articles—on the lower branches, the lighter articles above; ornament with glass balls of various colors, pictures, and other pretty things not intended for the children—put a tiny wax candle on the taper end of each branch, and light up in the evening. Have one this year, if you never had before; it will repay you to see the wild delight of the children.[5]

The steel engraving on the opposite page shows a tree very like the one described in 1860. It can easily be shifted from that bedroom scene to a table in the dining room, where you can festoon it with your wildest imagination: wafers, kringles, macaroons, New Years Cakes, Yule Dollies, and much more. You can make pine cones from the Speculatius dough, and roses with Rose Meringue. In short, as the nineteenth-century Pennsylvania Dutch minister Henry Harbaugh commented in his 1860s reminiscences about the preparations for Christmas: "What an endless baking of cookies—horses, rabbits, stars, hearts, birds and many shapes more. How richly the *Christkindel* rewarded the children. Then it was truly a pleasure to be a child. Would that I could be one again! I tell you, a childhood without Christmas is like an evening sky without stars, yes, like a world without a Saviour."[6]

Steel engraving from Peterson's Magazine for December 1866. (Roughwood Collection)

The Christmas Cook

ALMOND MACAROONS

1702

Refer to the photograph opposite the introduction.

YIELD: APPROXIMATELY 5 DOZEN MACAROONS.

3 egg whites
2 cups superfine sugar
3 teaspoons rosewater

2 tablespoons all-purpose flour
3½ cups finely chopped blanched almonds (see note)

Preheat the oven to 250°F.

Beat the egg whites until stiff and slightly dry. Gradually add the sugar, beating continuously, then add the rosewater. Mix the flour and almonds thoroughly, then add to the egg mixture. Beat vigorously until the batter is creamy.

Line baking sheets with baking parchment. Make *level* 1 tablespoon scoops of batter and space them evenly on the baking sheets. Allow for spreading. Dry for 45 to 50 minutes in the preheated oven or until the macaroons are fawn color. Let them cool on the baking parchment, then pull them off gently. They will stick if pulled off when hot. Store in airtight containers.

NOTE: You must begin with 1 pound of blanched almonds or the proportions will not work. Chop the nuts in your food processor in 2 equal batches, or you will chop part of the nuts too fine before the others are processed. For each 8 ounces of almonds, or 1¾ cups ground, allow 15 to 20 pulses on the food processor.

SOURCE: Samuel Nutt, "Savorall Rare Sacrets and Choyce Curiossityes" (Unpublished manuscript, Chester County: 1702–1737), 43. Collection of the Chester County Historical Society, West Chester, Pennsylvania. Quoted with the kind permission of the Society.

CHOCOLATE KISSES

1846

YIELD: 2 DOZEN KISSES.

3 egg whites
8 tablespoons superfine sugar
1 tablespoon all-purpose flour
¼ teaspoon olive oil

2 teaspoons vanilla extract
¼ cup cocoa
24 baking wafers (see note)

Preheat the oven to 250°F.

Beat the egg whites until stiff and slightly dry. Mix the sugar and flour and add to the eggs, beating continuously. Then add the olive oil and vanilla. Fold in the cocoa.

Place 24 baking wafers on an ungreased baking sheet. Take scoops of about 1 tablespoon each of the batter and put 1 scoop on each wafer. Or, put the batter in a pastry bag and make spiral kisses on the wafers. Dry in the preheated oven for approximately 1 hour and 15 minutes. Cool on racks, then store in airtight containers.

NOTE: Baking wafers are paper-thin white, edible rounds of wheat flour and starch that are used in baking many kinds of cookies instead of baking parchment. They are manufactured in West Germany by the firm of Franz Hoch, Miltenheim am Main. They are normally labeled *Back-Oblaten* or *gaufrettes*. They are available in some specialty shops in this country.

If you cannot obtain baking wafers, cut out 2-inch rounds of baking parchment and dust the top surface of each copiously with confectioners' sugar. Pull off the paper after the kisses have cooled.

SOURCE: *Turner's Improved Housekeeper's Almanac for 1846* (Philadelphia: Turner & Fisher, 1845), unpaginated.

Fancy Kisses (BELOW) made with a pastry bag, Illustrations from a turn-of-the-century cookbook. (Roughwood Collection)

Kisses at the End

GÂTEAU DE POMMES

1860

The recipe that I selected here came from the manuscript cookbook of Mary Hamilton Winebrenner, whose recipe for Raisiné appears in the previous chapter. Old-style gâteau de pommes was something like stiff apple butter, although rose colored. It took roughly 2 hours to make, and you knew it was done only from having made it several times, which is something of a catch-22 situation.

Later in the nineteenth century, Sarah Tyson Rorer came out with a much easier technique that she taught at her Philadelphia Cooking School. Where the old method fretted over pectin, Mrs. Rorer has substituted gelatin, and it works. I have blended Mrs. Winebrenner's recipe and Mrs. Rorer's into one and the result is extraordinarily good. The best part of it is that you can now take on Gâteau de Pommes without batting an eye, even in elaborate molds like the one used to make the gâteau on the opposite page.

YIELD: APPROXIMATELY 2 QUARTS, 10 TO 12 SERVINGS.

---

5 large tart apples (exactly 2 pounds peeled and cored, peels and cores reserved)
3 cups water or red currant juice
¼ cup lemon juice
3 cups sugar

Grated zest of 2 lemons
4 envelopes unflavored gelatin
4 drops oil of cinnamon (see note)
Strips of candied citron and slivered blanched almonds

Pare and core the apples. You *must* have 2 pounds at this point, so weigh the prepared apples. Place the peels and cores in a stewing pan with 3 cups of water or red currant juice —water will give you a green gâteau, red currant juice will give you a rose one. Cover the peels and simmer 15 minutes, then strain and reserve 2½ cups of liquid.

Chop the pared, weighed apples into small pieces and purée them in a food processor with the lemon juice. Purée until the texture of the apples resembles applesauce. Put the purée in a clean stewing pan with the sugar and grated lemon zest. Soften the gelatin with ½ cup of the reserved apple liquid. Add the rest of the liquid to the purée.

Cover and cook the purée for 15 minutes. Add the softened gelatin and boil hard for 2 minutes. Remove from the heat immediately and add the oil of cinnamon if you choose. Pour the hot apple batter into a 2 quart china mold or into several small ones and let

it cool. When cool, put it in the refrigerator to set overnight.

To remove the mold, dip it in warm water and turn it over onto the serving dish. Historically, the gâteau was ornamented with strips of citron and slivered almonds. The almonds were stuck into it like spines. Around the base of the mold it was customary to make a ring of custard. The recipe for Orange Cream (page 238) will serve this purpose very well. Or use the custard recipe that is the first part of Kentucky Cream on page 168.

NOTE: If you do not have oil of cinnamon, put 2 sticks of cinnamon in the pan with the peels and cores. Discard when you are finished cooking the peels.

SOURCE: Mary Hamilton Winebrenner, "Housekeeper's Book" (Unpublished manuscript, Harrisburg, Pa.: 1837—1879), unpaginated. Roughwood Collection.

FROM LEFT TO RIGHT: **spiral mold for Gâteau de Pommes, Dresden carp mold for New Years, capon mold (see the Lemon and Rum Jelly on PAGE 234), and a copper mold for Ribbon Jelly. All molds date from 1880–1900.**

An eggnog party in the South. From an 1870
wood engraving. (Roughwood Collection)

POPCORN BALLS

In his memoirs, John Jay Janney (1812–1907) noted that in northern Virginia popcorn was not known until about 1825, although roasting common corn had been done since the period of early settlement.[8] Real popping corn was a nineteenth-century addition to the general American menu and because of its cheapness, its popularity was almost universal. The *Cooking Club Magazine* described one way of preparing it in the days of open-hearth cookery: "A children's party can be enlivened by using the old-fashioned Dutch oven or skillet for the popper. When the corn is at its height of popping, set the vessel upon the floor and remove the lid. The popping grains will leap in all directions and cause a lively scramble among the children as they scamper about to secure them."[9] The grains that were left in the pan unpopped were called "old maids," or "grannies." They were ground in a coffee mill and served cooked for breakfast with cream and sugar.

YIELD: APPROXIMATELY 3 DOZEN SMALL BALLS.

3 quarts popped popcorn
1 cup unsulfured molasses

1 cup broken peanuts (optional)

Put the popcorn in a large work bowl. Heat the molasses in a saucepan and bring to a hard boil. Boil until it reaches the thread stage (230° to 234°F)—allow about 8 minutes. Immediately remove the molasses from the heat and pour it over the popcorn. Stir with a buttered batter stick. Butter your hands and mold into small balls about the size of an egg.

This produces a popcorn ball that has the flavor and texture of old-fashioned Cracker Jacks. Broken peanuts may be added to the popcorn if desired. If you stir the popcorn and syrup until the syrup cools, the popcorn will dry loose and can be served like Cracker Jacks.

SOURCE: Woman's Guild of Grace Church, *Capital City Cook Book* (Madison, Wisc.: Privately printed, 1906), 149.

Yule Tide Punch

This is a semifrozen punch that is loose and grainy in texture, much like granité. It may be served in scoops like Italian ice. I would also point out that in the cookbook from which this recipe was taken, the rum and wine had been eliminated and replaced with grape juice. I have restored the rum to the recipe because I think that is one of its distinctive qualities. It certainly improves the flavor.

YIELD: 1 GALLON, APPROXIMATELY 15 TO 20 SERVINGS.

2 quarts water
4 pounds sugar
2 pints pineapple juice (fresh, if possible)
1½ cups lemon juice
2½ teaspoons grated lemon zest
1 cup orange juice
2½ teaspoons grated orange zest
2 cups white grape juice, or 2 cups dry white wine, or 2 cups light rum

Mix the sugar with the water and boil 10 minutes. Add the pineapple juice and set aside to cool. When cool, add the lemon juice, lemon zest, orange juice, orange zest, and the grape juice, white wine, or rum. Put this into an ice cream freezer, or simply put it into a metal container, cover, and set in the deep freeze. When frozen, beat with a whisk (or feed small batches of it into your food processor) to smooth the texture, and pour into a punch bowl. Serve immediately.

SOURCE: Ladies' Aid Society of the Presbyterian Church, *The Tidioute Cook Book* (Tidioute, Pa.: News Steam Printing House, 1904), 188.

ORANGES FILLED WITH JELLY

1848

The woodcut on the opposite page shows a small centerpiece requiring 20 orange quarters (5 oranges), allowing one for the top piece.

YIELD: 40 QUARTERS, OR SUFFICIENT FOR 2 SMALL CENTERPIECES.

10 oranges
Boxwood or yew sprigs for garnish

FOR 1 RED LAYER:

6 tablespoons sugar
3 envelopes unflavored gelatin
1¾ cups boiling water
4 tablespoons lemon juice
Red food coloring

FOR 1 CLEAR OR ORANGE LAYER:

5 tablespoons sugar
3 envelopes unflavored gelatin
2 cups hot orange juice, or 1¾ cups
boiling water plus 3 tablespoons
lemon juice
Red and yellow food coloring (for
orange layer)

Clean each orange with a grapefruit spoon, working through a hole at the top no larger than a quarter. Remove everything, fruit and membranes. Then set the oranges in a muffin pan to keep them level while you fill them with gelatin.

You must prepare the layers of gelatin in separate batches because each layer must cool and set before you can make another. The number of layers is entirely up to you, but I think 3 or 4 look best.

To make a batch of gelatin for 1 red layer, mix the sugar and gelatin. Add boiling water, lemon juice, and red food coloring. For 1 clear or orange layer, mix the sugar and gelatin. Add hot orange juice or boiling water, lemon juice, and red and yellow food coloring, for the orange layer. Of course, if you want a clear layer, omit the coloring. As you put the gelatin into each orange, measure carefully, as for example, 4 tablespoons for the first layer. Put the oranges in the re-

Oranges Filled with Jelly, from an 1866 woodcut. The serving basket is made of pastry. (Roughwood Collection)

frigerator and cool until that layer has set. Then repeat the process with a different color gelatin, making certain that this layer also measures at least 4 tablespoons. By measuring, each layer will be even, although you must compensate for the fact that the orange is getting wider with each layer. Therefore, a middle layer may require 7 tablespoons instead of 4. Actually, this problem does not

crop up unless the oranges are very large— but you should be aware of it.

Once the oranges are filled and the gelatin is set firm, carefully slice the oranges into quarters with a very sharp knife. It sometimes helps to dip the knife blade in hot water if the gelatin does not seem to cut neatly. A firm, downward sawing action is usually successful. Arrange the slices in small pyramids on 2 fancy serving dishes and garnish with boxwood or yew between the slices, as shown in the old woodcut.

After you slice the oranges, you may want to brush the exposed edges of the rind with clear gelatin, especially if you plan to have the centerpiece stand out for any great length of time. This precaution will help keep the rind from discoloring and drying out. Otherwise, the slices will keep in the refrigerator several days. But I think they look best the day they are made.

SOURCE: Eliza Acton, *Modern Cookery*, ed. Sarah J. Hale (Philadelphia: Lea and Blanchard, 1848), 312.

LEMON AND RUM JELLY

1895

The model for this festive dish was calf's foot jelly (an aspic) flavored with white wine and lemon.[7] With the advent of commercial gelatin in the 1860s, this dish became much less expensive and far easier to make. This, in turn, encouraged mold manufacturers to increase the output and variety of shapes. Many gelatin firms also promoted molds with their product. Most of the fine, ornamental copper molds sold in this country during the nineteenth century were made in England. Sheffield was one of the centers of production.

The tinned copper capon mold on page 227 was made in the United States not only for gelatins, but for steamed puddings and ice creams as well. It was a popular mold for chicken cheese, a chicken meat aspic. I have used it, however, to make a capon with the Rum and Lemon jelly. The "bird" is garnished with truffles made of Raisiné and tiny candied crab apples. Playing games with food materials and shapes was popular with Christmas cooks in the Victorian era.

YIELD: 2 QUARTS, SUFFICIENT FOR 12 SERVINGS.

6 envelopes unflavored gelatin
2 cups sugar
1 quart boiling water

2 cups cold water
⅔ cup strained lemon juice
1 cup white rum

Mix the gelatin and sugar. Add the boiling water and stir until the gelatin and sugar are dissolved. Add the cold water. When the liquid is tepid, add the lemon juice and rum. Pour into a 2-quart mold or into several small molds and put in the refrigerator to set. Turn out right before serving by dipping the mold into warm water and turning it over onto the serving dish.

SOURCE: Mrs. Thomas L. Rosser, *Housekeepers' and Mothers' Manual* (Richmond, Va.: Everett Waddey Co., 1895), 431.

Lemon and Rum Jelly in the form of a capon is garnished with sliced "truffles" of Raisiné (PAGE 212–213), myrtle oranges, boxwood greens, and candied crab apples. The Glacé Fruits are glazed in the style of dripping ice.

HICKORY NUT MACAROONS

— 1877 —

*T*his excellent recipe comes to us from Philadelphia confectioner James W. Parkinson. He sold these at his famous restaurant on Chestnut Street.

YIELD: APPROXIMATELY 5 DOZEN MACAROONS

3 egg whites
2 cups superfine sugar
6 tablespoons all-purpose flour

4 cups finely chopped hickory nuts
(see note)

*P*reheat the oven to 250°F.

Beat the egg whites until stiff and slightly dry. Sift together the sugar and flour twice, then sift and fold this into the egg whites. Fold in the nuts and mix thoroughly. Using your hands, break off balls about the size of a walnut and roll them on the palms of the hands to make them perfectly round. Line baking sheets with baking parchment and set the balls of nut mixture on them. Dry in the preheated oven 55 to 60 minutes. These macaroons will puff as they dry in the oven. Cool completely on racks and store in airtight containers.

NOTE: It is necessary to have 1 pound of nuts for this recipe. Weigh them before chopping. You may chop them in a food processor. For each 8 ounces of nuts, allow 40 short pulses. Hazelnuts may be used instead, but the flavor of hickory nuts is unique.

SOURCE: *The Confectioners' Journal* 3 (July 1877), 17.

ICED GRAPES

1872

YIELD: SUFFICIENT FOR 1 STANDING CENTERPIECE.

4 pounds grapes
3 egg whites
Superfine sugar

Choose perfect bunches of grapes; discard any blemished grapes. Trim the bunches to the desired size, then, for convenience in hanging the grapes to dry, tie a string to the stem of each bunch. Be certain the string is tied securely.

Dip a paintbrush into the unbeaten egg whites and brush the grapes only enough to lightly moisten them. Dust liberally with superfine sugar. Touch up spots where the sugar misses and then hang the grapes to dry. Tie them to a clothesline or towel rack with the strings you have attached to the stems. When the sugar is dry, remove the strings and use the grapes in constructing the table centerpiece.

SOURCE: *Mrs. Winslow's Domestic Receipt Book for 1872* (New York: Jeremiah Curtis & Sons and John I. Brown & Sons, 1871), 31.

Victorian stand for iced fruit. From a wood engraving. (Roughwood Collection)

ORANGE CREAM
1850

YIELD: APPROXIMATELY 1½ QUARTS, 8 TO 10 SERVINGS.

¾ *cup sugar*
1 *cup orange juice*
¼ *cup lemon juice*
3 *teaspoons grated orange zest*

1 *quart milk*
3 *envelopes unflavored gelatin*
8 *egg yolks*

Put the sugar, orange juice, lemon juice, and orange zest in a saucepan and boil until a thick syrup forms. The syrup must literally "explode" with orange flavor or the cream will be bland.

Bring the milk to a boil, then reduce the heat and dissolve the gelatin in it. Beat the eggs to a cream, and whisk them into the warm milk mixture. Strain the orange syrup and add it to the milk mixture. Beat continuously over low heat until this thickens to a rich custard consistency.

Pour into syllabub glasses like those shown on the cover, serving cups, or a large china bowl. Cool in the refrigerator until set.

It should have a consistency somewhat like a mousse.

NOTE: This cream is a pale yellow in color, but the cream shown in the old chromolithograph on the opposite page is a very bright orange. It was customary to doctor the colors. A few drops of red and yellow food coloring will bring out the orange. The flavor can also be enhanced with orange flower water or orange extract. I hesitate to recommend orange extract because most of the commercial products I have tried are harsh and taste metallic, and I swear I can taste metal in the cream.

SOURCE: Mrs. Bliss. *The Practical Cook Book* (Philadelphia: Lippincott, Grambo & Co., 1850), 246.

SNOW PUDDING

In her *Housewife's Helper* (Cato, N.Y., 1898), Mrs. A. R. Pennell refered to this dish as Snow Drift, another of its many popular names.[10] It *does* look like snow, particularly on top.

YIELD: 1½ QUARTS, SUFFICIENT FOR 8 TO 10 SERVINGS.

1 cup sugar
½ cup lemon juice
3 envelopes unflavored gelatin

4 tablespoons cold water
2 cups boiling water or milk
3 egg whites

Dissolve the sugar in the lemon juice. Soften the gelatin in the cold water, then mix it with the sugar and lemon. Stir to eliminate lumps. Add the boiling water or milk. Whisk to completely dissolve all the gelatin; set aside to cool. When the pudding is cold, but not yet stiff, beat the egg whites to a froth. Add to the pudding, beating until the mixture has a frothy texture. Pour into a mold or large bowl, set in the freezer, but do not freeze. Once it is firmly set, put it in the refrigerator until needed.

Turn the pudding out of the bowl by dipping it in warm water, then turning the bowl over into the serving dish. A bowl will give the "snowdrift" shape depicted in the chromolithograph at right.

SOURCE: Marion Harland, *The Comfort of Cooking and Heating by Gas* (New York: Consolidated Gas Co., 1898), 70.

A small plateau with orange, vanilla, and strawberry creams surrounding Snow Pudding ornamented with sweetmeats. Chromolithograph, circa 1870. (Roughwood Collection)

ROSE MERINGUES

The use of roses as decoration on Christmas trees is a very old one, perhaps because the Rose of Sharon was one of the Biblical designations for Christ. We know that one of the earliest recorded Christmas trees, from 1597, was ornamented with roses of paper and silk. Later, in the eighteenth and nineteenth centuries, these paper roses also found their counterparts in sugarwork and meringue.

Georg Christoph Neunhöfer, in his 1848 *Das Neueste der Conditoreikunst* (Up-to-Date Confectionery), provided a hand-colored engraving to show what fancy rose meringues should look like. The meringue was put into a pastry bag with the tip one would use for making roses in icing. The roses were formed by starting at the center and working outward, petal by petal—a good way to get stiff fingers!

Home cooks rarely exhibited such patience, and judging from Miss Eliza Leslie's 1852 recipe, it was a lot easier to drop scoops of the meringue on baking parchment and let it go at that.

The right color was considered far more important. It was common practice to heighten the red with alkanet root, a herb once widely used in cosmetics. The drawback to the spirited red (some might go so far as to call it garish) was that if the meringues were in any way overbaked, they turned an insipid, lugubrious shade of rust, a watch point that should not be ignored when you attempt this recipe.

YIELD: APPROXIMATELY 4 DOZEN MERINGUES.

3 egg whites
⅔ cup confectioners' sugar
¾ teaspoon rosewater

4 to 6 drops red food coloring
1 tablespoon minced red rose petals
(see note)

Preheat the oven to 250°F.

Beat the egg whites until stiff. Sift in the sugar and beat again until thoroughly combined. Fold in the rosewater, coloring, and minced petals.

Form your meringues as roses, scoops, or in kiss shape (peaked spirals) on baking parchment spread on baking sheets. Set the meringues in the oven for 35 to 40 minutes, or until they have dried out. To test if they are done, take one out; it should not be wet in the middle. If you inadvertently remove a whole sheet of meringues from the oven before they are done, they will most likely sink,

and there goes all your work. The finished meringues should be deep pink or red, not brown or tinged with yellow.

NOTE: Do not use roses that have been sprayed. Rose sprays do not degrade like fruit and vegetable sprays and are therefore extremely unsafe for consumption. For the purposes of this recipe, organically grown damask roses are best.

SOURCE: Eliza Leslie, *New Receipts for Cooking* (Philadelphia: T. B. Peterson, 1852), 202.

Before inexpensive wire whisks became available in the nineteenth century, most home cooks used twig switches, horn forks, or chocolate mills (as shown here) to whip egg whites for meringues.

Kisses at the End

PEANUT MACAROONS

1850

Another old term for this confection is *groundnut cake.* Regardless of what one calls them, they are truly delicious. But be absolutely certain to use good peanuts, because one or two rancid ones in the batch will give everything an off flavor. I recommend using the blanched, unsalted peanuts that come in vacuum-sealed jars. You *must* weigh your peanuts because all of the proportions in this recipe are keyed to weight.

For a different, crisper texture, you may reduce the weight of the peanuts to 1 pound, but also take out 2 tablespoons of flour.

YIELD: APPROXIMATELY 6 DOZEN MACAROONS.

1¼ pound blanched, unsalted peanuts
6 tablespoons all-purpose flour

5 egg whites
2 cups superfine sugar

Preheat the oven to 250°F.

Put the peanuts in a food processor and chop them to a coarse meal texture. Add the flour and combine thoroughly. Beat the egg whites until very stiff, then fold in the sugar. Combine the peanut and egg mixtures. Drop the batter in lumps of about 2 teaspoons each on ungreased baking parchment and dry 40 to 45 minutes, or until light brown. Lift the macaroons with a spatula and cool on racks. Store in airtight containers.

SOURCE: Mrs. Bliss, *The Practical Cook Book* (Philadelphia: Lippincott, Grambo & Co., 1850), 195.

New Years Card, circa 1910. (Roughwood Collection)

Notes

ONE
BRINGING IN CHRISTMAS

1. Frances Boardman Crowninshield, ed., *Letters of Mary Boardman Crowninshield 1815–1816* (Cambridge, Mass.: Riverside Press, 1935), 30.

2. See Susan G. Davis, " 'Making Night Hideous': Christmas Revelry and Public Order in 19th Century Philadelphia," *American Quarterly* 34 (1982), 185–99.

3. J. S. Udal, "Mummers and a Dorset Version of the Mummers' Play of St. George," *Dorsetshire Folk-lore* (St. Peter Port, Guernsey: Toucan Press, 1970), 435.

4. E. Cobham Brewer, *Dictionary of Phrase and Fable* (Philadelphia: Claxton, Remsen & Haffelfinger, ca. 1875), 451.

5. William Woys Weaver, *Sauerkraut Yankees* (Philadelphia: University of Pennsylvania Press, 1983), 192.

6. John Brand, *Observations on Popular Antiquities* (London: Chatto & Windus, 1900), 283.

7. F. G. Payne, "Welsh Peasant Costume," *Folk Life* 2 (1964), 42–57.

8. *Lamb's wool* was also the name of wassail in Yorkshire and other parts of central England. See Peter Brears, *Traditional Food in Yorkshire* (Edinburgh: John Donald, 1987), 181.

9. Brand, *Observations,* 4.

10. William Woys Weaver, *America Eats: Forms of Edible Folk Art* (New York: Harper & Row, 1989), 74.

11. Bridget Ann Henisch, *Cakes and Characters: An English Christmas Tradition* (London: Prospect Books, 1984).

12. William Byrd, *The Secret Diary of William Byrd of Westover,* vol. 2, ed. Louis B. Wright and Marion Tinling (Richmond, Va.: Dietz Press, 1942), 28.

13. *The American Family Cook Book* (Boston: Higgins, Bradley & Dayton, 1858), 40.

14. George F. Reinecke, "The New Orleans 12th Night Cake," *Louisiana Folklore Miscellany 2* (April 1965), 45–54.
15. Sarah McCorkle Case, ed., *Letters from a Lady of Lancaster 1777–1797* (Lancaster, Pa.: Privately printed, 1931), 26.
16. Mordecai Noah, *Essay of Howard on Domestic Economy* (New York: G. L. Birch, 1820), 38–39.
17. Mrs. Bliss, *The Practical Cook Book* (Philadelphia: Lippincott, Grambo & Co., 1855), 270–71.
18. S. Minwell Tibbott, *Welsh Fare* (St. Fagans, Wales: Welsh Folk Museum, 1976), 51–53.
19. See "Red Flummery," *The Farm Journal 5* (June 1855), 167.
20. Hugo Stopp, ed., *Das Kochbuch der Sabina Welserin* (Heidelberg: Carl Winter/Universitätsverlag, 1980), 99.

TWO

HUMBUG PIE: HOW THE POOR BROUGHT IN CHRISTMAS

1. "From a Correspondent," *Christian Advocate and Journal* (New York), 17 April, 1844.
2. See Gerald L. Davis, "Afro-American Coil Basketry in Charleston County, South Carolina," ed. Don Yoder, *American Folklife* (Austin: University of Texas Press, 1976), 151–84.
3. George W. McDaniel, *Hearth and Home: Preserving a People's Culture* (Philadelphia: Temple University Press, 1982), 110.
4. W. Emerson Wilson, ed., *Plantation Life at Rose Hill* (Wilmington, Del.: Historical Society of Delaware, 1976), 56.
5. William Woys Weaver, *Sauerkraut Yankees* (Philadelphia: University of Pennsylvania Press, 1983), 161–62.
6. *Commemorative Biographical Encyclopedia of the Juniata Valley* (Chambersburg, Pa.: J. M. Runk & Co., 1897), 1311.
7. Charles Camp, "America Eats: Toward a Social Definition of American Foodways" (Philadelphia: Ph.D. Diss., University of Pennsylvania, 1978), 210.
8. Werner L. and Asa Moore Janney, eds., *John Jay Janney's Virginia* (McLean, Va.: EPM Publications, Inc., 1978), 80.
9. Wilson, *Plantation Life*, 414.
10. Samuel Lammott, "Journal: Store Account Book," Union Bridge, Carroll County, Maryland, 1841–1849, unpaginated.
11. James W. Parkinson, "Answers to Correspondents," *The Confectioners' Journal 3* (January 1878), 22.

THREE

MARTIN LUTHER'S CHRISTMAS TREE

1. The woodcut on this page was issued by the Lutheran Board of Publication as a frontispiece in a children's book called *Luthers Christ-Baum* (Philadelphia: Lindsay and Blakiston, 1855).
2. Thoroughly discussed in Kurt Mantel, *Geschichte des Weihnachtsbaumes* (Hannover: Verlag M. u. H. Schaper, 1975).
3. Thomas Scharf, *History of Western Maryland*, vol. 2 (Philadelphia: Louis H. Everts, 1882), 1280–81.
4. See, for example, Alfred L. Shoemaker, *Christmas in Pennsylvania* (Kutztown, Pa.: Pennsylvania Folklife Society, 1959). He discusses a full range of customs.
5. There is a gingerbread mold (HG 9341) in the collection of the Germanisches Nationalmuseum in Nürnberg that illustrates one of these decorated Christmas fronds, abundantly hung with candy cherries. Another popular name for this nonevergreen bush was *Zuckerbaum* (sugar tree). See also Rudolf Schenda, "Die Geschichte des Weihnachtsbaumes," in *Weihnachten in Vergangenheit und Gegenwart*, ed. Herbert Schwedt (Tübingen: Ludwig Uhland Instituts für Volkskunde/Universität Tübingen, 1964), 12–13.
6. See, for example, Albert Becker, "Pfälzer Weihnachtsbräuche," in *Pfälzisches Museum/Pfälzische Heimatkunde*, Heft 5/6 (1922), 149–50; Theodore Zink, "Weihnachten in der Pfalz," *Unser Pfalz: Beilage zur Pfälzer Volksboten* 12 (1923); and Ernst Christmann, "Name und Alter des Christbaumes in der Pfalz," *Oberdeutsche Zeitschrift für Volkskunde* 5 Jg./Heft 2 (1931), 81–87.
7. Rolf Kunze, "Die Volkskunst des Schnitzens im Erzgebirge," *Glück Auf: Beiträge zur Folklorepflege* (Schneeberg, DDR, 1984), Heft 7/8: 22–26.
8. Ingeborg Weber-Kellermann, *Das Weihnachtsfest* (Luzern/Frankfurt: C. J. Bucher, 1978), 107.
9. Schenda, "Die Geschichte," 12–13.
10. Fully discussed in Ernst Thiele, *Waffeleisen und Waffelgebäcke in Mitteleuropa* (Köln: Oda-Verlag, 1959).
11. A reliable analysis of Luther's actual relationship to Christmas may be found in Erika Kohler's *Martin Luther und der Festbrauch* (Köln/Graz: Böhlau Verlag, 1959).
12. "Confectionery for the Holidays," *Christian Advocate and Journal* (New York), 28 December 1865.
13. Karl Meissen, *Nikolauskult und Nikolausbrauch im Abendlande* (Düsseldorf: Druck und Verlag von L. Schwann, 1931), 217.
14. "Anniversary Festival of Saint Nicholas," *The Knickerbocker* 29 (January 1847), 83.
15. Helga Tenschert, *Engelsbrot und Eisenkuchen* (München/Wien/Zürich: BLV Verlagsgesellschaft, 1983).
16. J. Dyneley Prince, "The Jersey Dutch Dialect," *Dialect Notes* 3:6 (1910), 472.
17. Rose's translation of *De Verstandige Kock* is available under the title *The Sensible Cook: Dutch Foodways in the Old and the New World* (Syracuse, N.Y.: Syracuse University Press, 1989).

FOUR

THE PASTRY COOK'S COMPANION

1. Caroline Scott Harrison, *The Washington Cook Book* (New York: G. W. Dillingham, 1890), 217.
2. Frances, "Are Sweetmeats Indispensable?," *Christian Advocate and Journal* (New York), 20 September 1838.
3. For example, "To Clarify Sugar for Sweetmeats," *The Household Guide and Family Receipt Book* (Springfield, Mass.: C. D. Leet, 1867), 21.
4. *The Household* (Brattleboro, Vt.) 7 (March 1874), 62.
5. *The Household* (Brattleboro, Vt.) 7 (April 1874), 87.
6. *M'Makin's Model American Courier* (Philadelphia), 16 November 1850.
7. Joseph Burnett & Co., *The Housekeeper's Friend* (Boston: Forbes Co., 1879).
8. *The Household* (Brattleboro, Vt.) 7 (October 1874), 231.
9. Mrs. Bliss, *The Practical Cook Book* (Philadelphia: Lippincott, Grambo & Co., 1855), 195.
10. "Hints to Housekeepers" *The Household* (Brattleboro, Vt.) 7 (March 1874), 61.
11. *The Household* (Brattleboro, Vt.) 7 (May 1874), 111.
12. *The Confectioners' Journal* 7 (December 1881), 42.

FIVE

BEWARE OF CAMELS

1. Hannah Glasse, *The Art of Cookery* (London: Printed for T. Longman, 1796), 310.
2. *Christmas with the Girls* (Philadelphia: American Sunday School Union, 1875), 23–24.
3. *The Household* (Brattleboro, Vt.) 7 (September 1874), 205.
4. Hans Wiswe, *Kulturgeschichte der Kochkunst* (München: Heinz Moos Verlag, 1970), 211–12.
5. Thomas Cooper, ed., *The Domestic Encyclopedia*, 3 (Philadelphia: Abraham Small, 1821), 477.
6. John Y. Kohl, "Christmas Cookies—A Controversy, Proceedings of the Lehigh County Historical Society" 22 (1959): 79–164.
7. *The Family Receipt Book* (Pittsburgh: Randolph Barnes, 1819), 164.
8. One of the best European studies is Albert Walzer's *Liebeskutsche, Reitersmann, Nikolaus und Kinderbringer* (Konstanz/Stuttgart: Jan Thorbecke Verlag, 1963).
9. *The Confectioners' Journal* 25 (September 1899): 14.
10. J. H. Kuhlman, *Holiday Help* (Loudonsville, Ohio: J. H. Kuhlman, 1917), 18–19.
11. The interplay of these images is analyzed by Ernst Guldan in his *Eva und Maria* (Graz/Köln: Verlag Hermann Böhlaus Nachfolger, 1966).
12. *The Confectioners' Journal* 25 (January 1899): 110.
13. Helen R. Martin, *Tillie, A Mennonite Maid* (New York: Grosset & Dunlap, 1904).

14. Maria Sophia Schellhammer, *Das branden-burgische Koch-Buch* (Berlin/Potsdam: Johann Andreas Rüdiger, 1732), 353.
15. It was printed at Einsiedeln, Switzerland, by the firm of Benziger & Company, which began issuing these pictures in 1801.
16. Phillip V. Snyder, *The Christmas Tree* (New York: Viking, 1976), 26–27.
17. Discussed thoroughly by Christa Pieske in her *Das ABC des Luxuspapiers* (Berlin: Dietrich Reimer Verlag, 1983), 189–192.
18. J. J. Schilstra, *Prenten in Hout* (Lochem: De Tijdstroom by, 1985), 164–83.
19. One of the earliest appearances of the word *cookie* in print may be found in the New York *Daily Advertiser* for 20 March 1786.
20. J. H. Spitzbub of Philadelphia, for example, advertised a large variety of imported German Christmas goods, including Nürnberg toys, gingerbreads, and wooden horses in the *United States Gazette*, 9 November 1807.
21. There is a large collection of these molds in the collection of the Deutsches Brotmuseum in Ulm, West Germany.
22. *Allen's Supply Buyers News* (Chicago: J. W. Allen & Co., 1926), 3.
23. *Practical Housekeeping* (Minneapolis: Buckeye Publishing Company, 1884), 488.
24. *Good Housekeeping*, March 1915, 99.
25. *United States Gazette* (Philadelphia), 28 December 1840.
26. C. H. King, "Crackers and Biscuits," *Bakers' Helper* (January 1898), 37.
27. *The Original Buckeye Cook Book* (St. Paul: Webb, 1905), 83.

S I X

WHO SAID PLUM PUDDING?

1. *The Spring of Knowledge or The Alphabet Illustrated* (London: J. L. Marks, ca. 1835), unpaginated.
2. *The Confectioners' Journal* (January 1878), 21.
3. Mrs. Horace Mann, *Christianity in the Kitchen* (Boston: Ticknor & Fields, 1861), 67.
4. Frederick G. Bascom, ed., *Letters of a Ticonderoga Farmer* (Ithaca, N.Y.: Cornell University Press, 1946), 131.
5. For example, *The Downingtown American Republican* of 29 December 1812 complained that the legislators of Pennsylvania had adjourned unnecessarily for a two-week holiday if nothing else than to draw *"Three dollars* a day for eating Christmas pies." Three dollars a day was their salary—taxpayer's money of course.
6. *The Lancaster (Pennsylvania) General Hospital "Benefit" Cook Book* (Lancaster, Pa.: Conn & Slote, 1912), 75.
7. John Brand, *Observations on Popular Antiquities* (London: Chatto & Windus, 1900), 284.
8. See Mrs. Julia A. Carney, "Whisky Pickles," *The Household* (Brattleboro, Vt.) 7 (September 1874), 208.
9. Eliza Leslie, *Miss Leslie's Cook Book* (Philadelphia: T. B. Peterson & Brothers, 1881), 490. This is a later edition of her *New Cookery Book*.
10. See for example, Susan Coolidge's use of the term in her "Fortunes of a Saucer-Pie," *St. Nicholas* 3 (November 1875), 42–44.
11. "Christmas Keeping," *The New Monthly and Literary Journal* (Philadelphia) 2 (July-December 1821), 646.

12. See the introduction to the reprint of John Nott's *Cook and Confectioners Dictionary,* ed. Elizabeth David (London: Lawrence Rivington, 1980), 30.

13. Mary J. Barr, "The Christmas Pudding," *Cooking Club Magazine* 5 (December 1903), 554.

14. *Sunday Dispatch* (Philadelphia), 17 December 1848. The Alhambra was situated at Seventh and Walnut streets.

15. *The Household* (Brattleboro, Vt.) 7 (June 1874), 135.

16. *The Household* (Brattleboro, Vt.) 7 (September 1874), 205.

S E V E N

SUGAR ORNAMENTS AND EDIBLE TOYS

1. Nellie Eyster, *Sunny Hours* (Philadelphia: Duffield Ashmead, 1865), 189.

2. See for example, the German chromolithograph firms discussed in Christa Pieske, *Das ABC des Luxuspapiers* (Berlin: Dietrich Reimer Verlag, 1983).

3. *The Confectioners' Journal* 4 (October 1878), 24.

4. Katherine B. Johnson, "Christmas Bon-Bons," *Housekeeper's Weekly* 3 (3 December 1892), 12.

5. Lettice Arnold, "Her Booke. Given by the Lady Lett. G." (Herefordshire, England: 1638), unpaginated.

6. There is a small 16-page pamphlet history of clear toy molds by collector Albert C. Dudrear called *Clear Toy Candy: History—Mould Makers—Recipe* (York, Pa.: Privately printed, 1983). It contains photocopies of old catalogue price lists.

7. "Christmas," *The Post* (Philadelphia), 20 December 1828.

8. Jessup Whitehead, recipe 222 "Candy for Christmas Toys," *The Hotel Book of Fine Pastries* (Chicago: National Hotel Reporter, 1881).

9. "Two Old Recipes," *Confectioner and Baker* 6 (April 1901), 21.

10. James W. Parkinson, ed., *The Complete Confectioner* (Philadelphia: Leary & Getz, 1849), 89.

11. John Comly, *Comly's Reader and Book of Knowledge* (Philadelphia: Thomas L. Bonsal, 1850), 143.

12. Refer, for example, to C. Anne Wilson's *The Book of Marmalade* (London: Constable & Company, 1985), 30–37.

13. Eliza Allen Howland, *The American Economical Housekeeper* (Worcester, Mass.: A. S. Howland, 1850), 112.

14. Mrs. Frances Owens, *Cook Book and Useful Household Hints* (Chicago: American Publishing House, 1903), 394. This book first appeared in 1884.

EIGHT

KISSES AT THE END

1. Lettice Bryan, *The Kentucky Housewife* (Cincinnati: Shepard & Stearns, 1841), 292.
2. Catherine E. Beecher, *The Handy Cook Book* (New York: J. B. Ford & Co., 1873), 519.
3. See "Hänsel und Gretelhaus," in Carl Krackhart, *Neues Illustriertes Conditoreibuch* (Nordhausen: Heinrich Killinger, 1907), 224.
4. Margaret Graham, "Suggestive Recollections of Christmas Festivities," *Cooking Club Magazine* 18 (November, 1916), 49.
5. E. M. Biddle, "To Make a Christmas Tree," *The Farmer and Gardener* (Philadelphia) 3 (December 1860), 189.
6. Alfred L. Shoemaker, *Christmas in Pennsylvania* (Kutztown, Pa.: Pennsylvania Folklife Society, 1959), 97.
7. See for example, *The Family's Guide* (Cortland, N.Y.: C. W. Mason, 1833), 10.
8. Werner L. and Asa Moore Janney, *John Jay Janney's Virginia* (McLean, Va.: EPM Publications Inc., 1978), 25.
9. "Popcorn in the Home," *Cooking Club Magazine* 15 (March 1913), 57.
10. Mrs. A. R. Pennell, *The Housekeeper's Helper* (Cato, N.Y.: Privately printed, 1898), 79.

Bibliography

Acomb, Evelyn M. *The Revolutionary Journal of Baron von Closen, 1780–1783*. Chapel Hill: University of North Carolina Press, 1958.

Acton, Eliza. *Modern Cookery*, Sarah J. Hale, ed. Philadelphia: Lea and Blanchard, 1848.

The American Family Cook Book. Boston: Higgins, Bradley & Dayton, 1858.

Angerer, Josef. *Der Moderne Konditor*. Leipzig/Nordhausen: Heinrich Killinger, ca. 1914.

The Approved Recipe Book. Plainfield, N.J.: Printed and for sale by M. F. Cushing, 1839.

Barr, Mary J. "The Christmas Pudding." *Cooking Club Magazine* 5 (December 1903): 554–55.

Bascom, Frederick G., ed. *Letters of a Ticonderoga Farmer*. Ithaca, N.Y.: Cornell University Press, 1946.

Becker, Albert, "Pfälzer Weihnachtsbräuche." *Pfälzisches Museum/Pfälzische Heimatkunde* Heft 5/6 (1922): 149–50.

Beecher, Catherine. *The Handy Cook Book*. New York: J. B. Ford & Co., 1873.

Belden, Louise Conway. *The Festive Tradition: Table Decoration and Desserts in America, 1650–1900*. New York: W. W. Norton & Co., 1983.

The Bethlehem Cook Book. Bethlehem, Pa.: Times Publishing Co., 1900.

Biddle, E. M. "To Make a Christmas Tree." *The Farmer and Gardener* (Philadelphia) 3 (December 1860): 189.

Bliss, Mrs. *The Practical Cook Book*. Philadelphia: Lippincott, Grambo & Co., 1855.

Boyd, Mrs. Samuel Becket. *The Tennessee and Virginia Cook Book*. Knoxville, Tenn.: First Presbyterian Church of Knoxville, 1911.

Brand, John. *Observations on Popular Antiquities*. London: Chatto & Windus, 1900.

Braun, Jakob. *Die Nürnberger Lebkuchen*. Nurnberg: Im Selbstverlag, ca. 1890.

Brears, Peter. *Traditional Food in Yorkshire.* Edinburgh: John Donald, 1987.

Brewer, E. Cobham. *Dictionary of Phrase and Fable.* Philadelphia: Claxton, Remsen & Haffelfinger, ca. 1875.

Briggs, Richard. *The New Art of Cookery.* Philadelphia: W. Spotswood, R. Campbell, and B. Johnson, 1792.

Brody, Alan. *The English Mummers and Their Plays.* Philadelphia: University of Pennsylvania Press, 1970.

Bryan, Mrs. Lettice. *The Kentucky Housewife.* Cincinnati: Stereotyped by Shepard & Stearns, 1841.

Burnett, Joseph & Co. *The Housekeeper's Friend.* Boston: Forbes & Co., 1879.

Burton, William E. *Cyclopedia of Wit and Humor, of America, Ireland, Scotland, and England.* New York: D. Appleton & Co., 1857.

Byrd, William. *The Secret Diary of William Byrd of Westover, 1709–1712.* 2 vols. Edited by Louis B. Wright and Marion Tinling. Richard, Va.: Dietz Press, 1941 and 1942.

Camp, Charles. "America Eats: Toward a Social Definition of American Foodways." Philadelphia: Ph.D. Diss. University of Pennsylvania, 1978.

Carney, Julia A. "Whiskey Pickles." *The Homestead* (Brattleboro, Vt.) 7 (September 1874): 208.

Carter, Susannah. *The Frugal Housewife, or Complete Woman Cook.* Boston: Edes and Gill, 1772.

Case, Sarah McCorkle, ed. *Letters from a Lady of Lancaster 1777–1797.* Lancaster, Pa.: Privately printed, 1931.

Christian Advocate and Journal (New York), 16 November 1827, 17 April 1844, 28 December 1865.

Christmann, Ernst, "Namen und Alter des Christbaumes in der Pfalz." *Oberdeutsche Zeitschrift für Volkskunde* 5 Jg./Heft 2 (1931): 81–87.

Christmas Holidays; or, A Visit at Home. Philadelphia: American Sunday School Union, 1835.

"Christmas Keeping," *The New Monthly and Literary Journal* (Philadelphia) 2 (July-December 1821): 646.

Christmas with the Girls. Philadelphia: American Sunday School Union, 1875.

Coffin, Tristram P. *The Book of Christmas Folklore.* New York: The Seabury Press, 1973.

Comly, John. *Comly's Reader and Book of Knowledge.* Philadelphia: Thomas L. Bonsal, 1850.

Commemorative Biographical Encyclopedia of the Juniata Valley. Chambersburg, Pa.: J. M. Runk & Co., 1897.

Coolidge, Susan. "The Fortunes of a Saucer-Pie." *St. Nicholas* 3 (November 1875): 42–44.

Cooper, Dr. Thomas, ed. *The Domestic Encyclopedia.* 3 vols. Philadelphia: Abraham Small, 1821.

Corning, Mrs. W. H., "Christmas in the Far West." In *Cyclopedia of Wit and Humor,* New York, 1857), 440–43.

Cox, J. Stevens. *Mumming and the Mummers' Play of St. George.* St. Peter Port, Guernsey: Toucan Press, 1970.

Croly, Mrs. J. C. *Jennie June's American Cookery Book.* New York: The American News Company, 1874.

Crowninshield, Francis Boardman, ed. *Letters of Mary Boardman Crowninshield 1815–1816.* Cambridge, Mass.: Riverside Press, 1935.

Davidis, Henrietta. *Praktisches Kochbuch für die Deutschen in Amerika.* Milwaukee: W. Georg Bumler's Verlag, 1879.

Davis, Gerald, "Afro-American Coil Basketry in Charleston County, South Carolina." In *American Folklife,* edited by Don Yoder. Austin, Texas: University of Texas Press, 1976.

Davis, Susan G. " 'Making Night Hideous': Christmas Revelry and Public Order in 19th Century Philadelphia," *American Quarterly* 34 (1982): 185–99.

Dietrich, Mrs. C. E. *Family Cook Book of German Recipes.* Richmond, Va.: A. S. Kratz, 1914.

Dudrear, Albert. *Clear Toy Candy. History-Mould Makers-Recipe.* York, Pa.: Privately printed, 1983.

Ellesworth, M. W., and F. B. Dickerson. *The Successful Housekeeper.* Harrisburg, Pa.: Pennsylvania Publishing Co., 1883.

Engels, Mathias. *Das kleine Andachtsbild.* Recklinghausen: Verlag Aurel Bongers, 1983.

Eupel, Johann Christian. *Der vollkommene Conditor.* Weimer: Verlag von Bernhard Friedrich Voigt, 1840.

Every Lady's Book. New York: J. K. Wellman, 1846.

Eyster, Nellie. *Sunny Hours, or Child Life of Tom and Mary.* Philadelphia: Duffield Ashmead, 1865.

The Family Receipt Book. Pittsburgh, Pa.: Randolph Barnes, 1819.

The Family's Guide. Cortland, N.Y.: C. W. Mason, 1833.

Farley, John. *The London Art of Cookery.* London: Printed for J. Scatcherd and J. Whitaker, 1787.

Frances. "Are Sweetmeats Indispensable?" *Christian Advocate and Journal,* 21 September 1838.

"From a Correspondent. Letter No. XIX." *Christian Advocate and Journal,* 7 April 1844.

Gibson, Mrs. Charles H. *Maryland and Virginia Cook Book.* Baltimore: John Murphy & Co., 1894.

Girardey, George. *Höchst nützliches Handbuch über Kochkunst.* Cincinnati: J. A. James, 1842.

Glasse, Hannah. *The Art of Cookery, Made Plain and Easy.* London: Printed for T. Longman, 1796.

Gray, Nada. *Holidays: Victorian Women Celebrate in Pennsylvania.* Lewisburg, Pa.: Oral Traditions Project of the Union County Historical Society, 1983.

Greaser, Arlene, and Paul H. Greaser. *Cookie Cutters and Molds: A Study of Cookie Cutters, Turk's Head Molds, Butter Molds, and Ice Cream Molds.* Allentown, Pa.: National Advertising Manufacturing Co., 1969.

Gregory, Annie R. *Woman's Favorite Cook Book.* Chicago: Sold by subscription, 1902.

Guldan, Ernst. *Eva and Maria: Eine Antithese als Bildmotiv.* Graz/Köln: Verlag Hermann Böhlaus Nachfolger, 1966.

Hall, Mary Elizabeth. *Candy Making Revolutionized: Confectionery from Vegetables.* New York: Sturgis & Walton Co., 1914.

Harding, Anneliese. *The Edible Mass Medium.* Cambridge, Mass.: Reisinger Museum, Harvard University, 1975.

Harland, Marion. *The Comfort of Cooking and Heating by Gas.* New York: Consolidated Gas Co., 1898.

Harrison, Mrs. Benjamin. *The Washington Cook Book.* New York: G. W. Dillingham, 1890.

Harrison, Molly. *The Kitchen in History.* Reading, England: Osprey Publishing, 1972.

Hebel, J. P. *Alemannische Gedichte.* Carlsruhe: In Macklots Hofbuchhandlung, 1806.

Heeger, F. "Schlettstadt in Elsass, die Wiege des Weihnachtsbaumes." *Pfälzer Land* no. 13 (1932).

Henisch, Bridget Ann. *Fast and Feast: Food in Medieval Society*. University Park: Pennsylvania State University Press, 1978.

———. *Cakes and Characters*. London: Prospect Books, 1984.

Homespun, Priscilla (pseud.). *The Universal Receipt Book*. Philadelphia: Isaac Riley, 1818.

Hoofland's Almanac and Family Receipt Book for Everybody's Use. Philadelphia: Johnston, Holloway & Co., 1874.

Hooker, Richard J. *A Colonial Plantation Cookbook: The Receipt Book of Harriott Pinckney Horry, 1770*. Columbia, S.C.: University of South Carolina Press, 1984.

Hörandner, Edith. *Model: Geschnitzte Formen für Lebkuchen, Spekulatius und Springerle*. München: D. W. Callwey, 1982.

The Household Guide and Family Receipt Book. Springfield, Mass.: C. D. Leet, Pub., 1867.

Huling, Charles. *Revised American Candy Maker*. Philadelphia: Published by the author, 1908.

Howland, Eliza Allen. *The American Economical Housekeeper*. Worcester, Mass.: A. S. Howland, 1850.

Janney, Werner L., and Asa Moore Janney, eds. *John Jay Janney's Virginia: An American Farm Lad's Life in the Early 19th Century*. McLean, Va.: EPM Publications, Inc., 1978.

Johnson, Katherine B. "Christmas Bon-Bons." *Housekeeper's Weekly* 3 (3 December 1892): 12.

Just, Johannes. *Das Museum für Volkskunst Dresden*. Dresden: Staatliche Kunstsammlungen, 1977.

Kevill-Davies, Sally. *Jelly Moulds*. Guilford, England: Lutterworth Press, 1983.

King, C. H. "Crackers and Biscuits." *Bakers' Helper* 7 (January 1898): 137.

Kohl, John Y. "Christmas Cookies—A Controversy." *Proceedings of the Lehigh County Historical Society* 22 (1958): 79–96.

Kohler, Erika. *Martin Luther under der Festbrauch*. Köln/Gratz: Böhlau Verlag, 1959.

Krackhart, Carl. *Neues Illustriertes Conditoreibuch*. Nordhausen: Heinrich Killinger, 1907.

Krythe, Maymie R. *All About Christmas*. New York: Harper & Brothers, 1954.

Kuhlman, J. H. *Holiday Help: New Ideas for Christmas for Sunday Schools and Day Schools*. Loudonville, Ohio: J. H. Kuhlman, 1917.

Kunze, Rolf. "Die Volkskunst des Schnitzens im Erzgebirge." *Glück Auf: Beiträge zur Folklorepfledge* (Schneeberg, DDR) Heft 7/8 (1984): 22–26.

Ladies Aid Society of the Presbyterian Church. *The Tidioute Cook Book*. Tidioute, Pa.: News Steam Printing, 1904.

The Lancaster (Pa.) General Hospital "Benefit" Cook Book. Lancaster, Pa.; Conn & Slote, 1912.

Leslie, Eliza. *Directions for Cookery*. Philadelphia: Carey & Hart, 1848.

———. *New Receipts for Cooking*. Philadelphia: T. B. Peterson, 1852.

———. *Miss Leslie's New Cookery Book*. Philadelphia: T. B. Peterson, 1857.

———. *Seventy-Five Receipts*. Boston: Munroe & Francis, 1828. Also the edition of 1838.

Loofft, Marcus. *Nieder-Sächsisches Koch Buch*. Lübeck: Christian Iverson u. Co., 1778.

Lyford, Carrie Alberta. *A Book of Recipes for the Cooking School*. Hampton, Va.: The Hampton Normal and Agricultural Institute, 1921.

W. M. *The Compleat Cook*. London: Printed by E. B. for Nath. Brook, 1658.

Mann, Mrs. Horace. *Christianity in the Kitchen: A Physiological Cook Book.* Boston: Ticknor & Fields, 1861.

Malcomson, Robert W. *Popular Recreations in English Society 1700–1850.* Cambridge/London: Cambridge University Press, 1979.

Mantel, Kurt. *Geschichte des Weihnachtsbaumes.* Hannover: Verlag M. u. H. Schaper, 1975.

Martin, Helen R. *Tillie, A Mennonite Maid.* New York: Grosset & Dunlap, 1904.

Mason, Charlotte. *The Ladies' Assistant for Regulating and Supplying the Table.* London: Printed for J. Walter, 1787.

May, Anna. *Die kleine New Yorker Köchin.* New York: Verlag von E. Steiger, 1859.

McCulloch-Williams, Martha. "Christmas Cates." *Good Housekeeping Magazine* (December 1914): 763.

————. *Dishes & Beverages of the Old South.* Knoxville, Tenn.: University of Tennessee Press, 1988.

McDaniel, George W. *Hearth & Home: Preserving a People's Culture.* Philadelphia: Temple University Press, 1982.

Metamorphosis; or A Transformation of Pictures, with Poetical Explanations. Harrisburg, Pa.: G. S. Peters, 1843.

Myers, Mrs. Ella E. *The Centennial Cook Book and General Guide.* Philadelphia: J. B. Myers, Publisher, 1876.

Neues Gothaisches Kochbuch oder allgemeiner Küchen-Wirthschafter. Gotha: In der Ettingerschen Buchhandlung, 1804.

Neunhofer, Georg Christian. *Das Neueste der Conditoreikunst.* Heilbronn: C. Drechsler'sche Buchhandlung, 1848.

New American Cookery, or Female Companion. New York: D. D. Smith, 1805.

Noah, Mordecai. *Essays of Howard on Domestic Economy.* New York: G. L. Birch, 1820.

North Reformed Church. *Cooks in Clover.* Passaic, N.J.: Thurston & Barker, 1889.

Nott, John. *Cooks and Confectioners Dictionary.* Edited by Elizabeth David, London: Lawrence Rivington, 1980.

Nutt, Frederic. *The Complete Confectioner.* New York: Richard Scott, 1807.

Owens, Frances E. *Mrs. Owens' Cook Book and Useful Household Hints.* Chicago, Ill.: American Publishing House, 1903.

Parker, Deborah H., and Jane E. Weeden. *Indiana W.C.T.U. Hadley Industrial School Cook Book.* Indianapolis: Organizer Print, 1883.

Parkinson, James W., ed. *The Complete Confectioner, Pastry-Cook and Baker.* Philadelphia: Leary & Getz, 1849.

————. "Christmas 1875: Christmas Good Cheer." *The Confectioners' Journal* 2 (December 1875): 17–18.

————. "Christmas Good Cheer." *The Confectioners' Journal* 2 (December 1877): 20.

————. "Christmas Fruit Cake." *The Confectioners' Journal* (December 1881): 42.

Parloa, Maria, et al. *Choice Recipes.* Dorchester, Mass.: Walter Baker & Co., 1904.

Payne, F. G. "Welsh Peasant Costume." *Folk Life* 2 (1964): 42–57.

Pechstein, Klaus, and Ursula Ellwart. *Festliches Backwerk.* Nürnberg: Germanisches Nationalmusem, 1981.

Pennell, Mrs. A. R. *The Housekeeper's Helper.* Cato, N.Y.: Privately printed, 1898.

Pieske, Christa. *Das ABC des Luxuspapiers. Herstellung, Verarbeitung und Gebrauch 1860 bis 1930.* Berlin: Dietrich Reimer Verlag, 1983.

"Popcorn in the Home." *Cooking Club Magazine* 15 (March 1913): 57.

Porter, Mrs. M. E. *Mrs. Porter's New Southern Cookery Book.* Philadelphia: John E. Potter & Co., 1871.

Practical Housekeeping. Minneapolis: Buckeye Publishing Co., 1884.

Prince, J. Dyneley. "The Jersey Dutch Dialect." *Dialect Notes* 3 (1910): 459–84.

The Queen of the Kitchen: A Collection of Old Maryland Receipts for Cooking. Baltimore: Lucas Brothers, 1870.

Raffald, Elizabeth. *The Experienced English Housewife.* Philadelphia: Printed for Thomas Dobson, 1801.

Reinecke, George F. "The New Orleans 12th Night Cakes." *Louisiana Folklore Miscellany* 2 (April 1965): 45–54.

Rorer, Sarah Tyson. *Home Candy Making.* Philadelphia: Arnold & Co., 1886.

Rose, Peter. *The Sensible Cook: Dutch Foodways in the Old and the New World.* Syracuse, N.Y.: Syracuse University Press, 1989.

Rosser, Mrs. Thomas L. *Housekeepers' and Mothers Manual.* Richmond, Va.: Everett Waddey Co., 1895.

Rundell, Maria. *A New System of Domestic Cookery.* Philadelphia: Benjamin C. Buzby, 1810.

Sanderson, James M. *The Complete Cook. Plain and Practical Directions for Cooking and Housekeeping.* Philadelphia: Leary & Getz, 1849.

Schellhammer, Maria Sophia. *Das brandenburgische Koch-Buch.* Berlin/Postdam: Johann Andreas Rüdiger, 1732.

Schilstra, J. J. *Prenten in Hout: Speculaas-, taai- en dragantvormen in Nederland.* Lochem: De Tijdstroom by, 1985.

Schwedt, Herbert, et al. *Weihnachten in Vergangenheit und Gegenwart.* Tübingen: Ludwig Uhland-Instituts für Volkskunde/Universität Tübingen, 1964.

The Secretary's Guide, or Young Man's Companion . . . To Which Is Added the Family Companion. Philadelphia: Printed and sold by Andrew Bradford, 1737.

Segschneider, Ernst. *Festliches Backwerk im Jahreslauf Osnabrück: 20 Jahrhundert.* Osnabrück: Kulturgeschichtliches Museum Osnabrück, 1975.

Shoemaker, Alfred L. *Christmas in Pennsylvania: A Folk-Cultural Study.* Kutztown, Pa.: Pennsylvania Folklife Society, 1959.

Simmons, Amelia. *American Cookery.* Hartford, Conn.: Hudson & Goodwin, 1796.

Smith, Eliza. *The Complete Housewife.* Williamsburg, Va.: Printed and sold by William Parks, 1742.

Snyder, Phillip V. *The Christmas Tree Book.* New York: Viking, 1976.

The Spring of Knowledge or the Alphabet Illustrated. London: J. L. Marks, ca. 1835.

Stirnemann, Johannes. ". . . es duftet nach Zimt und Nelken: Zimtwaffeln und Waffeleisen." *Die Pfalz am Rhein* (Neustadt) Heft 4 (November 1987): 36–37.

Stowe, Harriet Beecher. *Poganuc People: Their Loves and Lives.* New York: Fords, Howard & Hulbert, 1878.

Tennent, Mrs. E. R. *House-Keeping in the Sunny South.* Atlanta, Ga.: James P. Harrison Co., 1885.

Tenschert, Helga. *Engelsbrot und Eisenkuchen mit Oblaten backen nach alten Rezepten.* München/Wien/Zürich: BLV Verlagsgesellschaft, 1983.

Thiele, Ernst. *Waffeleisen und Waffelgebäcke.* Köln: Oda-Verlag, 1959.

Tibbott, S. Minwell. *Welsh Fare.* St. Fagans, Wales: Welsh Folk Museum, 1976.

Turner's Improved Housekeeper's Almanac for 1846. Philadelphia: Turner & Fisher, 1845.

Tutweiler, Julia S. "St. Nicholas' Day in Germany." St. Nicholas 3 (December 1875): 97–103.

The Twelve Months of the Year. Concord, Mass.: John F. Brown, 1873.

Udal, J. S. Dorsetshire Folk-lore. St. Peter Port, Guernsey: Toucan Press, 1970.

Village Improvement Society. Book for the Cook: Old Fashioned Receipts for New Fashioned Kitchens. Bridgeport, Conn.: The Hurd & Taylor Co., 1899.

Walzer, Albert. Liebeskutsche, Reitersmann, Nikolaus und Kinder-Bringer. Konstanz/Stuttgart: Jan Thorbecke Verlag, 1963.

Warren, Nathan B. The Holidays: Christmas, Easter and Whitsuntide. New York: Hurd and Houghton, 1868.

Waschinski, Emil. Alte Schleswig-holsteinische Masse und Gewichte. Neumünster: Karl Wachholz Verlag, 1952.

Weaver, William Woys. America Eats: Forms of Edible Folk Art. New York: Harper & Row, 1989.

———. Sauerkraut Yankees. Philadelphia: University of Pennsylvania Press, 1983.

Weber-Kellermann, Ingeborg. Das Weihnachtsfest. Luzern/Frankfurt: C. J. Bucher, 1978.

Whitehead, Jessup. The Hotel Book of Fine Pastries. Chicago: National Hotel Reporter, 1881.

Widdifield, Hannah Hungary. Widdifield's New Cook Book. Philadelphia: T. B. Peterson & Bros., 1856.

Wilson, C. Anne. The Book of Marmelade. London: Constable, 1985.

Wilson, W. Emerson. Plantation Life at Rose Hill: The Diaries of Martha Ogle Forman 1814–1845. Wilmington, Del.: Historical Society of Delaware, 1976.

Winslow, Mrs. Mrs. Winslow's Domestic Receipt Book for 1869. New York: Jeremiah Curtis & Son and John I. Brown & Sons, 1868. Also the edition for 1872.

Wiswe, Hans. Kulturgeschichte der Kochkunst. München: Heinz Moos, 1970.

Woman's Guild of Grace Church. Capital City Cook Book. Madison, Wisc.: Privately printed, 1906.

Zink, Theodore, "Weihnachten in der Pfalz," Unser Pfalz: Beilage zur Pfälzer Volksboten (1923), no. 12.

MANUSCRIPT SOURCES

Arnold, Lettice. "Her Booke. Given by the Lady Lett. G." Herefordshire, England, 1638. Roughwood Collection.

Bern Academy. "Manuscript Account Book of Bern Academy." Berks County, Pennsylvania, 1870s. Library Company of Philadelphia.

Boothby, Frances. "Her Booke of Cockery." Essex, England, 1660. Wife or daughter of Sir Thomas Boothby. Roughwood Collection.

Haines, Hannah Marshall. "Receipt Book." Germantown, Philadelphia, 1811–1824. The Wyck Association, Philadelphia.

Lammott, Samuel. "Journal: Store Account Book," Union Bridge, Carroll County, Maryland, 1841–1844, with recipes added ranging into the 1850s. Roughwood Collection.

Lockwood, Carrie Ayres. Manuscript Cook Book. Norwalk, Connecticut, 1867. Collection of the Lockwood-Mathews Mansion, Norwalk, Connecticut.

Nutt, Samuel. "Savorall Rare Sacrets and Choyce Curiossityes," Chester County, Pennsylvania, 1702–1737. Collection of the Chester County Historical Society, West Chester, Pennsylvania.

Romeyn, Eliza Dodge. Manuscript Recipe and Poetry Book, Columbia County, New York, 1825. Roughwood Collection.

Winebrenner, Mary Hamilton. "Housekeeper's Book." Harrisburg, Pa., 1837–1879. Roughwood Collection.

Historical Illustrations

PAGE 236
Woodcut from *The American Agriculturalist* (December 1868), 449.

PAGE 237
Woodcut from Vydra & Bohuslav, *Preis Katalog* (Prague, June 1909), 146.

PAGE 239
Hand-colored engraving from *Cassell's Household Guide* (London: Cassell, Petter and Gilpin, circa 1870), frontispiece from volume 2.

PAGE 243
Chromolithograph New Years card, circa 1910. Roughwood Collection.

Index